T0355576

OVERCOMING THE BUSH LEGACY
IN IRAQ AND AFGHANISTAN

Also by Deepak Tripathi

Breeding Ground: Afghanistan and the Origins of Islamist Terrorism

Sri Lanka's Foreign Policy Dilemmas

Related Titles from Potomac Books

Getting Away with Torture:
Secret Government, War Crimes, and the Rule of Law
—*Christopher H. Pyle*

The Other War:
Winning and Losing in Afghanistan
—*Amb. Ronald E. Neumann (Ret.)*

After the Taliban:
Nation-Building in Afghanistan
—*Amb. James F. Dobbins*

How We Missed the Story:
Osama bin Laden, the Taliban, and the Hijacking of Afghanistan
—*Roy Gutman*

The Four Freedoms Under Siege:
The Clear and Present Danger from Our National Security State
—*Marcus Raskin and Robert Spero*

War and Destiny:
How the Bush Revolution in Foreign and Military
Affairs Redefined American Power
—*James Kitfield*

OVERCOMING THE BUSH LEGACY IN IRAQ AND AFGHANISTAN

Deepak Tripathi

FOREWORD BY JOHN TIRMAN

POTOMAC BOOKS, INC.
WASHINGTON, D.C.

Library of Congress Cataloging-in-Publication Data

Tripathi, Deepak.
  Overcoming the Bush legacy in Iraq and Afghanistan / Deepak Tripathi ; foreword by John Tirman. — 1st ed.
    p. cm.
  Includes bibliographical references and index.
  ISBN 978-1-59797-503-2 (hardcover : alk. paper)
  1. United States—Foreign relations—2001–2009. 2. United States—Foreign relations—Philosophy. 3. War on Terrorism, 2001– 4. Afghan War, 2001– 5. Iraq War, 2003– 6. Bush, George W. (George Walker), 1946– —Political and social views. 7. United States—Politics and government—2001–2009. 8. Conservatism—United States—History—21st century. I. Title.
  E902.T75 2010
  973.931—dc22

                                                      2009053315

Printed in the United States of America on 100% recycled paper.

Potomac Books, Inc.
22841 Quicksilver Drive
Dulles, Virginia 20166

First Edition

10 9 8 7 6 5 4 3 2 1

To all those innocent men, women, and children
who suffered on 9/11 and in the war on terror

Contents

Foreword

When George W. Bush was inaugurated president in 2001, the United States was widely perceived as a champion of human rights, sensitive to the aspirations of the global south, supportive of women's empowerment, fiscally sound and responsible, alert to and cooperative on global environmental challenges, and an honest broker in trying to resolve many of the world's chronic conflicts. The record was far from perfect, but this perception was the norm. Within only a year, the new president had disrupted or reversed each of those American assets. From there, the situation worsened: war in Iraq, killing one million; support for, or involvement in, other wars in the region; redoubled efforts to penetrate and scavenge in third world economies; a nearly complete denial of the scientific consensus on global climate change; an evangelical Christian approach to family planning in the developing world; and runaway budgets and tax cuts for the wealthy, while the financial sector was deregulated to the point of a near collapse of the U.S. and world economies in the autumn of 2008, a fitting conclusion to his presidency.

Bush was not sui generis, nor was he a junior replica of his father. Bush instead modeled himself after Ronald Reagan. Right down to the ranch he purchased shortly before entering office, where he, like Reagan, would clear brush on his frequent holidays, Bush posed as a man's man, a modern-day cowboy, simple and decisive. That he came from a blueblood New England family with degrees from Yale and Harvard would not be apparent from his

assumed Texan identity, but then, everything about the forty-third president
was a pretense. He was not a good student, he failed at nearly every business
enterprise his family's money entitled him to try, his military service in the
reserves was a sham, he was a wastrel until he supposedly found Jesus and
came to grips with his alcoholism (which Frank Rich noted as the only thing
he ever actually achieved), and his governorship in Texas was largely devoid
of accomplishment. His hero, Reagan, was much the same: a self-styled fron-
tiersman who had achieved little until he was elected governor of California,
and then defeated a failed president. He cut taxes for the rich; drove up budget
deficits intentionally, so money for social programs would be scarce; followed
a "doctrine" of war—proxy wars, in his case—that left millions dead; worked
against the empowerment of the weak and of women; perfervidly denied that
the Earth's health was at risk; and embraced dictators from apartheid South
Africa to Latin America to Pakistan. The principal difference between the two
men was that Reagan was a consummate politician, able to adapt to chang-
ing circumstances and opportunities, as with his embrace of Gorbachev and
détente when his presidency was shaken by the Iran-contra scandal. Bush had
none of Reagan's charm or his instinctive grasp of politics.

What links them, too, is the nearly thirty-year run of Republican right-
wing ideology, which both identified with and to some extent shaped and
which was shown irrefutably to be bankrupt by 2008; the two of them, "the
Gipper" and "W," are the bookends of that disaster. Bush, even more than Reagan, was the culmination and embodiment of that ideology, and with majori-
ties in Congress during most of his presidency (which Reagan never had), he
could enact the conservative agenda. A major piece of that agenda, common to
Reagan and the Republican right, was war—war in Afghanistan, war in Iraq,
support for Israel's wars in Lebanon and Gaza, saber rattling over Georgia,
harsh confrontation with North Korea and Iran, an aggressive attitude toward
China, and a mentality that always emphasized military solutions over those
afforded by diplomacy, governance, cooperation, and the other arts of politics
and persuasion. Nothing illustrated this more than the war on terror.

Bush ignored the threats issued by Osama bin Laden until it was too
late, and to compensate for what should have been an impeachable breach
of responsibility, Bush set off on the war on terror, the "if you're not with

us, you're against us" mode of leadership, a dictum easily imagined to spring from the mouth of a celluloid gunslinger. The war, as Deepak Tripathi so ably demonstrates in this well-argued book, involved two direct invasions, plus a worldwide dragnet for possible "evil doers," a severely tightened system of immigration, the detention of thousands of Muslims and Arab Americans in the United States, expulsion of several hundreds, prosecutions of alleged plots (very few of which appeared to be remotely threatening), and rousing popular sentiments against the Arab world as well as anyone in the United States who questioned this anti-Muslim jeremiad.

The strategy of war against Afghanistan and Iraq was, as Tripathi rightly focuses on, the centerpiece of this global war on terror. Both failed to diminish the incidences of actual political violence and very likely increased the number of people who sought to commit acts of violence. Indeed, the attacks or plots in Madrid, London, and elsewhere are all linked to outrage over civilian deaths caused by U.S. and UK interventions in Afghanistan and Iraq. The number of Muslims in particular, seeing these wars as purely anti-Islam, who are alienated from the United States, is surely in the many millions. At the same time, Bush supported Israel's war against Lebanon in 2006 (which Condoleezza Rice unaccountably described as "the birth pangs of a new Middle East") and the Israeli siege of Gaza, culminating in the high-casualty military action in the winter of 2008–9, while refusing to acknowledge the democratic standing of Hezbollah and Hamas, sent a message of gross injustice in the U.S. handling of this most sensitive conflict. Meanwhile, the wars in Afghanistan and Iraq have resulted in roughly one million casualties (or more), 5 million displaced from their homes in Iraq alone, and a near-collapse of the health system, education, and the other rudiments of a functional and caring society.

By any standard, these actions have been catastrophes. By the end of his presidency, Iraq remained in a parlous state, politically riven and unstable; Afghanistan was actually worsening, and there was the distinct possibility that the Taliban would return (and seize control of Pakistan too); and a right-wing government was brought to power in Israel with vows that Bush had approved vastly expanded Israeli settlements on Palestinian land. The cacophony about American torture practices suddenly seized the headlines, proving what Bush had denied for years. More revelations, harming America's reputation, will surely issue forth to further expose this incompetent and immoral presidency. The financial crisis has already weakened America's standing and may permanently undermine its premier status in the global economy.

Deepak Tripathi is well qualified to explore these grisly but important topics. He spent twenty-three years as a distinguished correspondent and editor with the BBC, and he reported from many of the venues the Bush administration would affect so directly—Afghanistan, where Tripathi set up the Kabul bureau for BBC; Syria; Pakistan; and elsewhere—and he has contributed to a broad range of periodicals on these topics as well. His journalistic skills and experience are apparent in this terse treatment, but a moral passion that too often journalists leave at the door is also woven into the analysis, to the benefit of the readers. It would be a fool's errand to consider Bush in the usual "objective" mode of pluses and minuses because it can be said, nearly without fear of later reassessment, that Bush's foreign policy, his assault on civil liberties, his economic policies at home and abroad, and his neglect of environmental and development needs worldwide place his eight years as the most glaring failure of any presidency, certainly since the 1920s and, in the scale of the damage he has wrought, perhaps without equal in American history. That we now have Deepak Tripathi's sharply reasoned account of this catastrophe—its origins, its unfolding, and its consequences—will serve as a powerful warning for generations to come.

JOHN TIRMAN
MIT CENTER FOR INTERNATIONAL STUDIES

Acknowledgments

There are numerous individuals who have made this book possible. Some knew what terrible things they did on September 11, 2001, and in its aftermath. Their numbers are small in comparison to the innocent who suffered as a result of the 9/11 attacks on the World Trade Center and the Pentagon and those who became victims of the massive retaliation called the war on terror during the eight long years of George W. Bush's presidency. It is impossible to know all the names. But I remember them and am profoundly sorry for their sufferings. This book would not have been written without them.

I cannot thank Hilary Claggett of Potomac Books enough. Her enthusiasm, support, and understanding have been vital. I am grateful to other members of the Potomac staff for working so hard on this project.

I am particularly indebted to Clive Stafford Smith, who offered all I asked for. His book, *Bad Men: Guantánamo Bay and the Secret Prisons*; his interviews; and his international legal action charity, Reprieve, helped me comprehend the extent and depth of violations of the law and human rights made in the name of fighting terrorism.

I have benefited from the wisdom, generosity, and friendship of many people: Noam Chomsky, who continues to write ceaselessly on state and corporate behavior and matters of public concern; Philippe Sands, QC, whose books and talks on law, torture, and human rights have been invaluable; Peter Linebaugh, whose work *The Magna Carta Manifesto: Liberties and Commons for All* was an essential part of my education as I wrote the manuscript; Paul Rogers, whose columns on conflict and security are always worth reading; Ahmed Rashid, whose knowledge about the Taliban, al Qaeda, Pakistan, and Afghanistan is unrivaled.

Among the many think tanks and organizations I would like to acknowledge are the American Civil Liberties Union, Amnesty International, Human Rights Watch, the Avalon Project of Yale Law School, and the National Security Archive of George Washington University. I also acknowledge the help I received from the Bush Files, official documents made available by Paul O'Neill, the treasury secretary for the first two years of President George W. Bush's term. These documents and Ron Suskind's website, *The Price of Loyalty* (http://thepriceofloyalty.ronsuskind.com), were important resources.

Other vital sources were the Secret Orcon log of interrogation of detainee 063, obtained and published by *Time* magazine and the *New Yorker*, which brought accounts of abuse at Iraq's Abu Ghraib prison into the public domain. I am also grateful to Rick Shenkman of George Mason University. He has been generous with his time and has placed my articles on the reputable History News Network, which he edits. I'd also like to thank Michael Albert and the staff of *Z Magazine*; my BBC colleagues and friends, who keep building the remarkable archive that is BBC News Online; and Ramzy Baroud, Bev Conover, and Chris Moore for their support and friendship.

Last but not least, I am grateful to my wife, Archana, for her unstinting support and dedication to whatever I do. It is her book too.

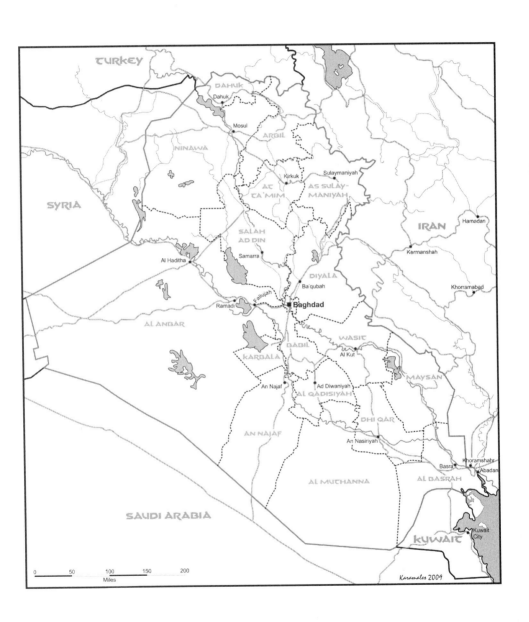

TURKEY

DAHUK

Dahuk

Mosul

ARBIL

NINAWA

SYRIA

Kirkuk · Sulaymaniyah

AT
TA'MIM

AS SULAY-
MANIYAH

IRAN

Hamadan

SALAH
AD DIN

Kermanshah

Al Haditha

Samarra

Khorramabad

DIYALA

Fallujah · Ba'qubah

Ramadi

Baghdad

AL ANBAR

WASIT

BABIL

KARBALA

Al Kut

MAYSAN

An Najaf

Ad Diwaniyah

AL QADISIYAH

DHI QAR

AN NAJAF

An Nasiriyah

Khoramshahr

Basra

Abadan

AL MUTHANNA

AL BASRAH

SAUDI ARABIA

KUWAIT

Kuwait
City

0   50   100   150   200
Miles

Karamales 2009

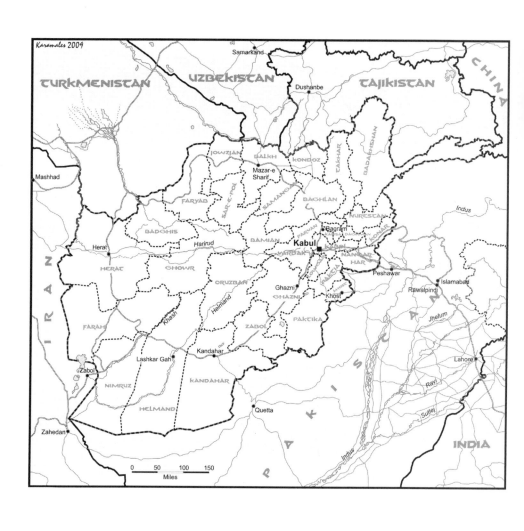

Prologue

We learn from history that we learn nothing from history.
—George Bernard Shaw

The inaugural decade of the twenty-first century is captured in images that will forever live in the annals of history to remind future generations about how a period that began with so much promise turned out to be so violent and disappointing.

Giant aircraft crash into the Twin Towers of the World Trade Center on September 11, 2001. Explosions and fires make gaping holes in the buildings. The skyscrapers turn to dust as they collapse. New Yorkers near the scene, distraught and bewildered, run for cover, and chaos follows. Collapsed buildings smolder for days, even weeks, as shock turns into rage and a determination to exact revenge. The large space where the Twin Towers once stood lies empty, attracting visitors from other parts of America and abroad. Grief-stricken relatives and friends of the three thousand who perished on 9/11 stand disoriented with cards bearing the names of the deceased. These images are widely available—on the Internet, in public libraries, and in museums across America. News organizations reproduce them as and when they need.

Then, there are images, buried deep in the military archives of the Pentagon and other U.S. government agencies. They tell the story of death and destruction in Afghanistan wreaked since the invasion of that country in

1

October 2001. Whether they show precision targeting or reckless killing depends on which side one stands. Documented civilian deaths in Afghanistan in the first six months of the war alone, from October 7, 2001, to March 31, 2002, are greater in absolute terms than the number killed on 9/11. The figures can be interpreted in different ways. The average number of innocent civilians killed in the U.S.-led bombing was just under fifty per day—roughly equivalent to thirty thousand American civilians, or as many as eleven World Trade Center attacks.[1] Afghanistan's soil has been soaked in blood since 9/11. The conflict progressively spread, the bloodshed continues.

B-52 warplanes drop two-thousand-pound cluster bombs. AC-130 gunships attack a farming village, killing almost a hundred civilians. A Pentagon official says, "The people there are dead because we wanted them dead." Why? Because they were Taliban sympathizers. When the U.S. defense secretary, Donald Rumsfeld, is asked, he does not want to talk about it. An odd-job man, Mohammed Raza, is on his way back to his house, near Jalalabad airport. A cruise missile meant to hit a Taliban facility goes astray and lands next to him. As it explodes, shrapnel pierces his neck, leaving him paralyzed. A bomb dropped from high altitude kills a hundred people in a village in the northern province of Kunduz. Mohammad Rasul describes how he pulled eleven bodies out of the rubble and buried them. He could do no more. Having fled his home, he is now a refugee.

Operation Shock and Awe is launched against Saddam Hussein in March 2003. Baghdad is hit by an endless stream of cruise missiles and bombs. Over fifteen hundred will be launched in the next twenty-four hours. The Pentagon in Washington proudly presents pictures of huge explosions, fireballs rising high up in the sky, filling it with thick dark smoke. Americans all across the country watch these images on their television screens and burst into loud applause. After days of intense bombardment, during which the Iraqi infrastructure is destroyed, a crowd cheers as U.S. Marines pull down the statue of Saddam Hussein in Baghdad's main square. This image is shown around the world for months.

Five years on, in Karma, a town near Fallujah, America is about to hand over security to the Iraqi government. Under the gaze of the occupation forces, a suicide bomber enters a municipal building and blows up scores of people, including American soldiers and himself. Human body parts lie under the smoldering rubble; the building is utterly destroyed. It is the third local government target in Anbar Province hit in a week. There are no foreign cameras to record the carnage, but images of horrific violence will forever live in the minds of locals who witnessed it. Foreign journalists are embedded with the occupation force units, their freedom to cover the war from all sides seriously hampered. From Shock and Awe through sporadic attacks on the occupation forces to full-scale civil war. A state of nature exists in Iraq—a condition in which violence rules and life is nasty, brutish, and short.

The shame of Abu Ghraib prison is uncovered in images of naked prisoners, the faces of some hooded, others covered in excrement. Ferocious dogs terrorize them. Iraqis are heaped on each other. Their American tormentors sit on top of the piles or gesticulate. Pictures that make their way to media outlets are a fraction of those that actually exist. Most are buried, if not destroyed. In any case, what happened inside the prison is too ghastly to discuss at length. Meanwhile, in the Guantánamo Bay detention camp, off the Florida coast, images of shackled prisoners in orange uniforms, their captors still holding them, their bodies stooping, walk slowly, taking each step reluctantly. As the world's revulsion grows, these images are quietly withdrawn from circulation by the Bush administration's information machinery. Guantánamo was invented as a model by America. It is no more.

The collapse of Soviet communism around 1990 and the rapid march of globalization were supposed to usher in a new era of peace and prosperity not seen in the twentieth century. But the West became focused, some would say too much so, on economic regeneration through market expansion. And it showed a tragic reluctance to engage anymore in the world's trouble spots, where the Cold War had been fought with a vengeance through clients. As the new century arrived, the West did not realize the unintended consequences of its change of policy. The march of globalization had gone too far— to China and India, which helped the rich world with cheaper goods and services in the short run, but also helped these rapidly emerging economies to become future rivals. The devastated battlegrounds that had little or nothing to offer were left abandoned.

When the rich world embarked on the journey to take its manufacturing and services to cheaper labor markets, it was letting a genie out of the bottle. Those who blame India and China for the growing demand for oil and the commodity's volatile prices miss the point.[2] These and other emerging countries make a large proportion of the consumer goods that Americans and Europeans use and thus will inevitably consume more energy. There is a second unavoidable consequence of this trend. Rising incomes of skilled workers mean growing middle classes in the emerging economies. People in these nations are fed more, receive better health care, live longer, and have more consumer goods—a consequence far more preferable than the widespread disease and famine of the past.

In September 2007 the former chairman of the U.S. Federal Reserve, Alan Greenspan, acknowledged that the invasion of Iraq in 2003 was largely about oil. Coming from someone who had worked under four presidents, including George W. Bush, the statement blew the cover from the U.S. occupation of Iraq.[3] A senior British military officer and an adviser to the Coalition Provisional Authority in Iraq after the invasion, Brig. Jim Ellery, put it more bluntly in a talk at London University. The war has helped to head off "the tide of Easternization"—the shift in power toward China and India.[4]

This book is an attempt to make sense of the "war on terror," the sweeping and simplistic label given by George W. Bush to the central project of his presidency. In the wake of the 9/11 attacks, it was a military operation against al Qaeda and the Taliban regime that had given it sanctuary in Afghanistan. The Taliban were removed from power. But al Qaeda and Taliban leaders went into hiding, only to transform themselves into a looser, more flexible international network, and this led to expansion of U.S. counterterrorism operations worldwide. From the outset, the global war against terrorism was directed at al Qaeda and its associates, but not at other non-Islamic organizations such as the Tamil Tigers of Sri Lanka or Christian, Jewish, and Sikh religious groups or nationalist groups around the world.

Next came the invasion of Iraq in March 2003. Weapons of mass destruction (WMDs), which America and Britain claimed Iraq had, could not be produced by the coalition after Saddam Hussein's overthrow. And no credible evidence of a link between his secularist regime and al Qaeda could be found. The 9/11 Commission, created under congressional legislation, said it found no "collaborative relationship" between the two, even though U.S. vice president Dick Cheney had insisted that the evidence was "overwhelming."[5] From Iraq, the Bush administration turned its attention to Iran, Syria, and, to a lesser extent, North Korea. The government in Pyongyang conducted an underground nuclear test in October 2006 and is thought to possess both nuclear and chemical weapons. Yet, to the astonishment of many, Bush announced in June 2008 that America would remove North Korea from the terrorist blacklist after it gave up details of some of its nuclear activities and ceremoniously blew up a cooling plant. Four months later, the United States duly executed its intention. Such was the pressure on Bush to ensure a legacy in the last few months of his presidency.

Much was made of America's mission to introduce democracy in the Middle East. However, friendly regimes in countries such as Saudi Arabia and Egypt, where oppression is routinely used, were left to get on with it. Suspects abducted by the CIA across the world were sent there to be interrogated under torture. Governments around the world readily adopted the rhetoric that was the centerpiece of the Bush administration. The American Civil Liberties Union expressed alarm over the continuing march toward a surveillance culture:

> It doesn't require some apocalyptic vision of American democracy being replaced by dictatorship to worry about a surveillance society. There is a lot of room for the United States to become a meaner, less open and less just place without any radical change in government. All that's required is the continuation of trends that have continued unimpeded in recent years.[6]

Among the trends mentioned were powerful new technologies, weakening privacy laws, the war on terror, and warrantless spying on citizens. All this happened under the pretext of national security. Unprecedented pressure from the executive greatly upset the system of checks and balances enshrined in the U.S. Constitution. And the executive came to be dominated by an oligarchy. The aim of this book is to trace the journey undertaken by George W. Bush during his eight years in the White House and assess its undeniable impact on the world.

1

ANATOMY OF NEOCONSERVATISM

> Nearly all men can stand adversity, but if you want
> to test a man's character, give him power.
> —Abraham Lincoln

President George W. Bush was not a subtle politician. His personal charm and Southern directness attracted many Americans and helped him win two elections to the White House. Each time he also had a stroke of luck. The Bush victory in November 2000 was one of the most controversial—and disputed—presidential election results in U.S. history. Just five Electoral College votes separated George W. Bush from his Democratic opponent, Al Gore. The state of Florida, with twenty-five electoral votes, gave that victory to Bush. Overall, Bush received half a million fewer popular votes than Gore. The legal battle after the election reached the U.S. Supreme Court, which decided that the recount of ballots by hand in Florida was unconstitutional and the Republican secretary of state of Florida could certify the result.

The Florida vote count that gave George W. Bush the victory was so controversial because his brother, Jeb, was governor of the state. The secretary of state, Katherine Harris, was not only a member of Governor Jeb Bush's cabinet, she was also the cochair of George W. Bush's presidential campaign in the state. In the end, a majority of just 537 popular votes out of a total of nearly

6 million ballots cast in Florida decided the result. It was certified by Bush's close ally, and a recount by hand was declared unconstitutional in a U.S. Supreme Court dominated by conservative judges.[1] There were allegations that the result was manipulated in favor of George W. Bush.[2]

Four years later, it was Bush's war on terror that, despite serious doubts among its critics, convinced America it was not the time to reject an incumbent president. A majority thought that George W. Bush should have a second term to see the country through the military campaigns he had launched in Afghanistan and Iraq and anything else he might do as part of his war on terror. The 2004 presidential campaign was particularly nasty. The neoconservatives who ran the Bush campaign focused on national security. George W. Bush was portrayed as a decisive leader; his Democratic rival, Senator John Kerry, was a "flip-flopper."[3] One of Kerry's slogans, "Strong at Home, Respected in the World," drew accusations that Kerry would pay more attention to domestic concerns than to America's defense.[4] Questions were raised about the legitimacy of the medals Kerry had been awarded during his military service in Vietnam.[5] Kerry stood little chance, and Bush won a second term in the White House.

A president who has served eight years in office is bound to leave a legacy. The single issue that, above all, defines the legacy of George W. Bush is the war on terror, which he pursued relentlessly during all but a few months of his presidency. It is tempting to suggest that the nature of American foreign policy under his administration was the consequence of the 9/11 attacks on the United States, for the invasions of Afghanistan and subsequently of Iraq came after those attacks. But this explanation provides no more than a convenient, and not entirely accurate, context to the war on terror. In truth, it illustrates a fundamental characteristic of the Bush presidency: an uncomplicated view of the world and America's role in it.

George W. Bush's presidency represents an era of the most aggressive U.S. foreign policy since Ronald Reagan's presidency in the 1980s. It will be remembered for its unilateralist character, demonstrated by the decision to pull out of the Kyoto Protocol on climate change in March 2001 and the invasion of Iraq in March 2003. America failed to convince the community of nations, even many of its allies, that Iraq had weapons of mass destruction and that the invasion and dismantling of the Iraqi state system was legal.[6] The declared purpose of the military campaign, to overthrow Saddam Hussein, was to make the world a safer place by eliminating the weapons of mass destruction that Iraq supposedly had. The result was a dismembered state in which non-state armed groups fought the occupation forces and each other. The dismantling of the Iraqi state destroyed the balance of power in the Gulf region and enhanced the status of Iran.

The 9/11 attacks would almost certainly have led to retaliation against the Taliban by any American administration. However, the scope of American ambition under Bush was something else. The campaign to overthrow the Iraqi regime of Saddam Hussein followed, Iran and Syria came under growing pressure, and there were warnings of military action against Iran. In the end, the Bush administration stopped short of direct military action against the Iranian regime for two reasons: the U.S. occupation forces had already become bogged down in Afghanistan and Iraq, and the American public was growing more skeptical about open-ended war without an identifiable enemy.

An enterprise of such magnitude cannot be undertaken without an ideological commitment to match it. The victory of George W. Bush in the November 2000 election was achieved on a tide of neoconservatism, ironically after a period of unprecedented economic growth during the Clinton administration. Scandals surrounding the personal life of President Clinton contributed significantly to the Bush victory. Clinton's moral crisis meant a boost for the religious Right, and the shift in public opinion away from the Democrats led to the defeat of Vice President Al Gore.

THE PROJECT

The ideological vehicle used to get George W. Bush elected to the White House in November 2000 was the Project for the New American Century (PNAC). Several of its founders were close to Bush and secured key positions in his first administration.[7] The PNAC was set up in early 1997, soon after President Clinton began his second term. Its founding members clearly had the 2000 election in mind. America was in the midst of an unparalleled economic renaissance, but criticisms of President Clinton and his wife, Hillary, were growing in the wake of controversies involving their personal lives and business dealings.[8]

From the outset, the neoconservatives sought to link domestic controversies surrounding the Clinton administration to what they described as a drift in American foreign and defense policy. While domestic critics focused on the personal conduct of Bill and Hillary Clinton, the Project for the New American Century attacked the president's agenda for economic recovery. The implication was that Clinton's economic program had a cost—weaker defense. Opponents accused him of "living off the capital," meaning both military investments and foreign policy achievements of previous Republican administrations.[9] The neoconservatives complained that the essential elements of the Reagan administration's success seemed to have been forgotten. Those elements were described as a "military that is strong and ready to meet both present and future challenges," a foreign policy that "boldly promotes American principles abroad," and national leadership that accepts America's "global responsibilities abroad." By implication, the neoconservative political machine depicted the Clinton-Gore administration as weak and inept.

The neoconservatives of the late 1990s were successors to the American Right of the previous decade and the Reagan-Bush presidency. The new generation was more energetic and aggressive. The Soviet empire had collapsed, so the United States no longer had to be everywhere around the globe to compete with communism. The neoconservatives could be selective, which made them more unilateralist.

Aware that the United States stood "as the world's pre-eminent power," the new conservatives were determined to "shape a new century favorable to American principles and interests." They believed that America had to be prudent in how it exercised power but could not avoid the costs associated with the exercise of its global responsibilities. They claimed America had a right to play a vital role in Europe and the oil-rich Middle East. The alternative, they said, would be inviting challenges to the country's fundamental interests, for the "history of the twentieth century should have taught us that it is important to shape circumstances before crises emerge." The underlying message was that the United States would intervene when it chose and where it chose if a neoconservative became president.

The new generation of conservatives declared their intentions well in advance. First, they said they would spend a lot more on defense and modernization of the armed forces "to carry out America's global responsibilities." Second, they would "strengthen ties with democratic allies and challenge regimes hostile to America's interests and values." The new political Right was clearly in search of like-minded allies committed to its ideology at a time when the North Atlantic Treaty Organization (NATO) was unsure of its role in the post-Soviet world. Third, they said they would promote "the cause of political and economic freedom abroad." Finally, they would preserve and extend "an international order friendly to our security, our prosperity, and our principles."

There was an unmistakable message of a more interventionist America in the new conservative program, which referred back to "Reaganite policy of military strength and moral clarity." But the ambition of the new Right went further—"to build on the successes of the past century and to ensure our security and our greatness in the next." From the beginning, neoconservative associations like the Project for the New American Century believed that American power was absolute in its potential and that its use was inevitable.

AMERICAN POLITICAL RIGHT: COMPOSITION, CHARACTER, AND AGENDA

At this point, I want to discuss the general disposition of new conservatism to help us examine the presidency of George W. Bush—or, at the very least, his victory and first term—in context. In broad terms, it is an ideological movement representing a range of political and social organizations that can be divided into two streams: neoconservatism and the religious Right. On one hand, there are new conservatives whose rise in the late 1990s can be attributed to the rebirth of the coalition that came together under Ronald Reagan twenty years before, even though the origins of the Reaganite political-religious alliance go back to the unsuccessful presidential bid of Barry Goldwater against Lyndon Johnson in 1964. Many leading figures of the neoconservative movement were younger politicians and thinkers who had been out of power during the Clinton presidency.

There are significant differences within the other stream, the American Christian Right, ranging from Lutheranism and Catholicism to the more conservative evangelical, Pentecostal, and fundamentalist churches. The differences between evangelicals and more moderate Christians are easier to identify on social issues. Moderate right-wingers tend to be less vehement in their opposition to abortion, stem cell research, and homosexuality and less staunch in their support of the death penalty. At the other end of the religious Right are those whose views on marriage, women's rights, abortion, the death penalty, and homosexuality are extreme.

White evangelical voters account for more than 20 percent of the American electorate. Their overwhelming support for George W. Bush was largely responsible for his success in the presidential elections. He received 68 percent of the white evangelical vote in the 2000 election and 78 percent four years later.[10] One of the most controversial personalities of the religious Right, evangelical preacher-politician Rev. Pat Robertson, has called feminism a "socialist, anti-family political movement that encourages women to leave their husbands, kill their children, practice witchcraft, destroy capitalism and become lesbians."[11] In 1998 Robertson claimed that acceptance of homosexuality could result in hurricanes, earthquakes, and terrorist attacks.[12] In the wake of the outcry after these remarks, he returned to the topic and, quoting from the Bible, sought to justify them.

The mass movement of neoconservatives and conservative Christians responsible for electing George W. Bush president has three main characteristics: a strong belief in America's power and right to exercise that power, conviction in the superiority of Judeo-Christian values, and a strongly pro-Israel and anti-Muslim agenda. The rhetoric of another leading figure on the American right, Bill O'Reilly, is also worth mentioning. During a radio discussion about an opinion poll showing that most Iraqis did not see American troops as liberators and wanted them to leave the country, O'Reilly told listeners that he had "no respect" for the Iraqi people; they were a "prehistoric group," and the lesson from the Iraq War was not that America should intervene in the Muslim world again, but that it should "bomb the living daylights out of them."[13] His support for coercive techniques to extract information at detention centers such as the one at Guantánamo Bay and for trials in military tribunals and his opposition to offering the detainees protection under the Geneva Conventions is well documented. The rhetoric of people like Robertson and O'Reilly cannot be dismissed as irrelevant and unrepresentative. Both command huge audiences through their television and radio broadcasts. Many aspects of the war on terror illustrate the place such views had in the Bush administration.

The overall disposition of the Bush administration reflected the prevailing belief across the new political Right that American power was unlimited and unaccountable and the United States could decide unilaterally whether, when, and to whom an international treaty would apply.[14] The essence of such a mind-set is "we will do it because we can." In this respect, there was considerable unity of purpose across the neoconservative spectrum. It was driven by a domestic political agenda. Foreign policy was an instrument to satisfy the conservative coalition at home for the sake of power.

There cannot be much argument about U.S. supremacy in terms of its economic and military strength, and the United States will exercise its power around the world. Indeed, it is desirable, even necessary, that America do so in a world that suffers from many natural and man-made calamities. Here, I want to discuss the manner in which that power is exercised and, to understand the difference between the new Right and the rest, one needs to appreciate the distinction between influence and control. Influence originates from a desire to persuade others by means of soft power, which has a much better chance of keeping the autonomy and honor of others intact. Control is necessarily aimed at imposing America's will elsewhere to get precise, predetermined results, often by the use, or threat, of direct military intervention.

Where the balance between the two is lost and there is too much reliance on one or the other, there are unexpected consequences. The new Right that dominated the Bush presidency was instinctively militaristic, despite events forcing several of its leading lights—Donald Rumsfeld, Paul Wolfowitz, and John Bolton—out of office.[15] Wolfowitz, in particular, had been a longtime advocate of the preemptive use of military force and had assembled a highly assertive team of senior officials in the Pentagon, especially after September 11, 2001. By February 2002 the hawks were confident enough to openly announce their intention in Iraq after invading Afghanistan.

In a newspaper interview, Wolfowitz said the United States "could not wait for proof beyond a reasonable doubt" because, when there was a possibility of weapons of mass destruction being used, to wait for proof was "fundamentally intolerable."[16] The decision to invade Iraq proved to be a colossal miscalculation. Weapons of mass destruction were not found. The legacies of the Iraq War include a fragmented nation split along ethnic and sectarian lines; regional powers, namely Iran and Syria, that are stronger than before; and an available sanctuary in Iraq, similar to that in Afghanistan, for local and foreign non-state groups.

The hawks surrounding George W. Bush were staunch supporters of Israel. Several were Jewish themselves. Irving Kristol, a founder of neoconservatism, who is also Jewish, justifies support of Israel with his assertion that the United States will "inevitably feel obliged to defend a democratic nation under attack from non-democratic forces." That is why, Kristol claims, America came to the defense of Britain and France in World War II and that is why "we feel it necessary to defend Israel today, when its survival is threatened."[17]

It is true that the United States played a crucial role in decolonization after World War II. American pressure was responsible to an extent for British withdrawal from India in 1947—an historic event that extended freedom to colonies in other parts of the world. However, the onset of the Cold War complicated the picture. As the race for influence between America and the Soviet Union became fierce, we also saw the United States intervene against democratic governments because it suited the American objective to contain communism. The coups by the CIA and British intelligence against Prime Minister Mohammad Mosaddeq of Iran in 1953, Prime Minister Patrice Lumumba of Congo in 1961, and President Salvador Allende of Chile in 1973 are just some of the examples.

America has allied itself with military and civilian dictatorships at the expense of democracy on other occasions as well, for example, with successive military regimes in Pakistan in preference to India, with the regime of the shah of Iran, and with the Saudi royal family. The Saudi regime is one of the most oppressive in the world but also one of America's closest allies. There is a large al Qaeda presence in Saudi Arabia. Yet, Bush described Iran, not Saudi Arabia, as part of the "axis of evil." Clearly America's national interests, oil, and access to strategic waterways are more compelling reasons for alliance than democracy.

In his 2006 State of the Union address, President Bush acknowledged that America was addicted to oil imports from unstable parts of the world.[18] In a study of U.S. dependence on Middle Eastern oil, Ian Rutledge provided an illuminating analysis. Rutledge wrote, "America's love affair with the car is leading to a relentless drive for energy security, at any cost—even war." He argued that the American invasion of Iraq was neither about "freedom" or "democracy," nor was it a plot to "steal Iraq's oil." Rather, it was an attempt to establish a compliant and dependable oil protectorate in the Middle East that would guarantee the rapidly rising demand from America's "hyper-motorized consumers."[19]

Rutledge challenged denials in America and Britain that the invasion of Iraq was launched in pursuit of oil. In 2006 he pointed out that millions of people around the world believed that oil was indeed the most important reason for the war. More than half of all passenger vehicles sold in America each year were large sports utility vehicles or other light trucks. No more than 4 percent of all Americans traveled by public transport to work, and over 15 percent of all workers were employed in automobile-related industries. Rutledge described the car as "the lynchpin of an oil economy."[20]

NEOCONSERVATISM: AN EXPANSIONIST IDEOLOGY

One of the most distinctive aspects of neoconservative ideology is a tendency toward expansionism. It manifests itself in a desire to push for steady economic growth on the domestic front. Abroad, the same expansionist tendency translates into an aggressive foreign policy backed by military strength. This tendency was obvious as early as 1992, when Paul Wolfowitz, the third-highest ranking civilian official at the Pentagon, drafted a controversial policy document, arguing for aggressive foreign policy.[21] After moving into the White House in 2001, George W. Bush adopted policies very similar to those recommended by Wolfowitz almost ten years before.

In the post-Soviet world, America's primary objective was to prevent the reemergence of a new rival that could generate global power. Most important among the regions where the United States would not tolerate opposition were Western Europe, the former Soviet Union, the Middle East, and East Asia. Wolfowitz cited three additional objectives in his document. First, the

United States had to convince potential competitors that they need not aspire to a greater regional or international role or pursue a more aggressive posture to protect their legitimate interests. Second, it had to account sufficiently for the interests of advanced industrial nations to discourage them from challenging American leadership. Third, America had to maintain the mechanisms for deterring potential competitors from even aspiring to a large regional or global role. Other American objectives abroad, according to Wolfowitz, were safeguarding U.S. interests, promoting American values, and, if necessary, taking unilateral action. The document did not mention taking collective action through the United Nations.

The scale of these ambitions made a much bigger foreign policy role for the state inevitable. At the same time, the neoconservatives supported tax cuts to stimulate economic growth, which meant a reduced economic role for the state. How could both be achieved? The new conservatives thought they had a solution. They did not mind creating budget deficits from time to time, as they believed economic growth would generate more revenues in the end, turning deficits into surpluses.[22] However, the eight years of the Bush presidency proved otherwise. According to the Historical Tables issued by the Office of Management and Budget, America had a surplus of $236 billion in the fiscal year ending in September 2000, less than four months before Bush took office in January 2001. In September 2004, eighteen months after the invasion of Iraq, the U.S. budget had sunk into a deficit of $413 billion. In the last full budget year during the Bush presidency, ending on September 30, 2008, there was an estimated deficit of $410 billion. The financial system in America and the rest of the world was in turmoil. Governments of the industrialized countries and emerging nations like China and India were pumping trillions of dollars into their economies, in deep crisis.

At the end of July 2008, the White House revised the deficit forecast for 2009, when President Bush would no longer be in office, to over $480 billion, excluding $80 billion in war costs. This forecast also did not account for the more than $225 billion borrowed from the Social Security Trust Fund. The real budget deficit, therefore, which Bush's successor was expected to inherit in 2009, would approach $790 billion.[23] The total public debt had passed the $10 trillion mark on September 30, 2008. The total cost of the Iraq War in its first five years was estimated to be $3 trillion to the United States and a similarly colossal amount to the rest of the world.[24]

As I have already suggested, it is a myth that the Bush administration's conduct was determined by the events of September 11, 2001. Let us look at the evidence. Bush was inaugurated as the forty-third president in January 2001 with Donald Rumsfeld soon to become his secretary of defense. Within a few weeks, Rumsfeld had made the administration's intentions clear. In a memo to senior officials, he called for a massive increase in military spending—eight months before the 9/11 attacks. The memo had the same message promoted by Wolfowitz in his policy document back in 1992. Wolfowitz was now Rumsfeld's deputy.

Rumsfeld repeated Wolfowitz's warning of the risk to U.S. security from small- to medium-sized states.[25] He mentioned Russia, China, Iran, Iraq, and North Korea among them. The first two were too big to take on. The last three were described by President Bush as the "axis of evil" in his State of the Union address on January 29, 2002. The term "axis of evil" was subsequently used to justify the war on terror. Rumsfeld claimed that additional spending totaling $334 billion would be required by 2007 to raise the U.S. military to the level it had been in 1992—the last year of the previous Republican administration, which had been headed by George H. W. Bush. And this money did not include the cost of the projects like missile defense that Bush Jr. wanted.

There was no mention of Afghanistan or al Qaeda in the Rumsfeld memo, suggesting that they were not of great concern to him. Instead, there was an obsession with the idea that there was imminent threat to American security from other rogue states such as Iran, Iraq, and North Korea, which were developing weapons of mass destruction. And Rumsfeld's priority was to prevent these countries from acquiring nuclear, chemical, and biological weapons.

The 9/11 attacks went against the neoconservative dogma that small- and medium-sized states, rather than non-state groups, posed a threat to U.S. security. Al Qaeda members who launched the attacks had entered America through normal channels, implanted themselves, and used ordinary knives to hijack passenger aircraft before crashing them into the World Trade Center and the Pentagon. Vehicles full of explosives were used in the previous al

Qaeda attack on the World Trade Center in 1993 and in the U.S. embassy bombings in Nairobi and Dar es Salaam in 1996. And, we should not forget the 1995 Oklahoma City bombing, for which two white members of a home-grown antigovernment militia were responsible.[26]

Neoconservatives who secured key positions in the Bush administration in January 2001 had a clear goal: to impose America's will in strategic locations anywhere, above all in the Middle East. Iran and Iraq had to be prevented from playing a role in the region that was not in tune with U.S. interests. There is evidence that the White House had begun considering plans for a post-Saddam Iraq within days of George W. Bush's inauguration.[27] Preemptive action was an integral part of the new strategy. The attacks on September 11, 2001, were a deviation that made the invasion of Afghanistan to overthrow the Taliban regime inevitable. But those events were not going to derail the Bush administration's long-term goal.

The neoconservatives in Bush's administration explained their dogma in terms of enforcement of freedom, democracy, and human rights, if necessary, by regime change from outside.[28] In fact, the dogma concealed America's twin interests—cheap oil and the defense of Israel—both driven by domestic considerations. For the new generation of Republicans, a strong coalition of the religious Right and the pro-Israel lobby was of fundamental importance for securing power after eight long years in opposition. With the Bush victory in 2000, the United States got probably the most pro-Israel president since the creation of the Jewish state. As long as Israel was secure and dominant in the Middle East, America would play a major role in the region and access to oil would be assured.

However, the new Republicans were not content with this. They were determined to take direct military action in Iraq, overthrow Saddam Hussein, and install a compliant regime. With 115 billion barrels of proven oil reserves, Iraq had the second-largest oil deposits in the world.[29] Fewer than twenty of eighty oil fields had been developed, and there had been no new exploration for years because of UN sanctions. Iraq also had significant reserves of natural gas, virtually all undeveloped. In Saudi Arabia, America's most reliable supplier, the royal family's hold on power was under growing threat from al Qaeda. Control over Iraq would guarantee the supply of oil if the Saudi oil supply was suspended as a result of political upheaval. The hawks who dominated the first Bush administration saw Iraq as a prime target.[30]

Bush ordered the invasion of Iraq in March 2003, without UN approval and despite strong international opposition. By the end of the Bush presidency, it was clear that the cost of invading Iraq had been very high. The lives of hundreds of thousands of Iraqi civilians and soldiers of the Iraqi and occupation armies had been lost, the Iraqi infrastructure had been destroyed, millions of Iraqis had been displaced, and there had been widespread human rights abuses and enormous damage to America's reputation around the world. When George W. Bush ordered the invasion of Iraq, the price of oil was around $40 a barrel. It reached a record of over $145 in 2008, before it collapsed in the global economic recession.

This brings to mind a quote by Martin Luther King Jr.: "Nothing in the world is more dangerous than sincere ignorance and conscientious stupidity." When both are in abundance, it is a catastrophe.

2

WITH US OR WITHOUT US

Problems cannot be solved at the same level of
awareness that created them.
—Albert Einstein

George W. Bush had been president less than eight months when America came under attack on September 11, 2001. Nothing particularly unusual had happened in the intervening months. The political storm over his controversial victory had subsided, and the Democrats were reconciled to spending the next four years in opposition. On social issues, Bush had announced restrictions on federal aid to women seeking abortions and increases in aid for religious institutions.

These announcements raised protests from liberal and moderate groups, which had been expected to oppose the Bush administration's conservative agenda. America's decision in March 2001 to withdraw from the Kyoto Protocol on climate change initially generated criticism abroad and disappointment from environmentalists at home. However, most had already acknowledged that the issue of climate change would have to be revisited at a later stage, under another U.S. administration.

The events of September 11 shattered the sense of normality. At 9:30 a.m., President Bush gave a brief speech about the attack on the World Trade

Center during a visit to an elementary school in Sarasota, Florida. He cut short his stay with this brief address, in which he announced that there had apparently been a terrorist attack on the United States. Two planes had crashed into the World Trade Center, and there had been casualties. He had to return to Washington immediately. It was a national tragedy, but terrorism would not succeed. America would hunt down those who had committed this act.[1]

At the end of an extraordinary day, Bush went on television to address the nation. Both towers of the World Trade Center had fallen, and the Pentagon building was still burning. There was no immediate count of casualties, but they were thought to be in the thousands. The most urgent task was to rescue as many victims as possible from the debris. Hospitals in New York and Washington were full of the dead and wounded. Anxious relatives and friends desperately tried to find out what had happened to their loved ones. The business of government had all but come to a halt, and the stock markets in the United States and abroad had closed. A climate of shock, mixed with fear and confusion, prevailed everywhere.

All these emotions were understandable as Americans struggled to comprehend the enormity of what had happened. But Bush's rhetoric in his television address reflected deep anger and strong retribution to come. An attempt to set America apart from the rest of the world seemed to be under way. Bush told Americans that their way of life, their very freedom, had come under attack and that lives had been ended by "despicable, evil acts of terror." He spoke of "unyielding anger" at the attempt "to frighten the nation into chaos and retreat."

Bush said the country had witnessed the very worst of evil because America was the "brightest beacon of freedom and opportunity in the world." He announced that the search for those behind the attacks had begun and they would be brought to justice. Then came the most telling part of his statement. He said that no distinction would be made between those who committed the acts and those who harbored the attackers; he was determined to win the "war against terrorism."[2] It was the first time he used the phrase, which would soon enter the political lexicon. The scene was set for America not only to retaliate against al Qaeda and the Taliban regime in Afghanistan, but to go beyond, with no apparent limits.

In the following days and weeks, the administration explained what the war would look like. Bush said the 9/11 attacks were a declaration of war against America. Osama bin Laden was a prime suspect, but those "who house him, encourage him, provide food, comfort and money" were also on notice. It was a war against all evil-doers and barbaric people who attacked America and those who helped them. There were other terrorists in the world—"people who hate freedom." They, too, would be hunted down.[3]

The events of 9/11 had taken the United States by surprise. However, several elements of the American response came from the neoconservative vision of the world that had evolved in the 1990s when President Clinton was in the White House and the Republicans were out of power. George W. Bush and his advisers saw the world as divided into two camps, just as it had been in the Cold War between the United States and the Soviet Union. This time, though, the confrontation was between America and the Islamic fundamentalists, between the civilized world and barbarism, freedom and tyranny. Bush promised "a monumental struggle of good versus evil, but good will prevail."[4]

With these remarks, America's imperial moment had arrived. Almost ten years before, President George H. W. Bush had spoken of a new international order following the collapse of the Soviet bloc. But his defeat to Bill Clinton, who was averse to using American military force, put an end to the possibility of a move in the direction Bush Sr. envisaged. Clinton's goal was to reduce America's colossal budget deficit, downsize the military, and rebuild a strong peacetime economy.[5] In 2001 the George W. Bush administration was determined to reshape the Middle East to suit America's interests forever.[6] It had Iraq and Iran in sight, but the events of 9/11 made it necessary to start in Afghanistan.

The history of al Qaeda attacks showed that the network used explosives in large quantities in areas of high population to cause maximum casualties. Even the 9/11 attackers were not equipped with weapons of mass destruction. They used knives to hijack planes before crashing three of them into the World Trade Center and the Pentagon. These attacks were so devastating because of intelligence and security failures and because the hijackers were ready to die. To extend the war to Iraq, and possibly other states, it was necessary for

the Bush administration to go beyond terrorism to weapons of mass destruction. It was the route to America's hegemony in the oil-rich Middle East.

THE BUSH DOCTRINE

In his 2002 State of the Union address, Bush declared that, after Afghanistan,
the second goal of the United States was to prevent regimes that sponsored
terrorism from threatening with "weapons of mass destruction."[7] This was a
significant departure from his central message up to this point. The way was
open for action against recognized regimes in addition to the Taliban, who
were almost totally isolated.[8]

For the first time, Bush used the term "axis of evil" to describe Iran, Iraq,
and North Korea. He named Iran for aggressively pursuing weapons of mass
destruction and exporting terrorism; Iraq for continuing to flaunt its hostility
toward America, supporting terrorism, and keeping its chemical and nuclear
programs hidden from "the civilized world"; and North Korea for developing
nuclear weapons while starving its citizens. Bush said these regimes had been
quiet since 9/11, but he knew their true nature.

The speech deliberately blurred the division between the threat posed by
al Qaeda and "weapons of mass destruction," a vague term that would allow
the administration to implement its grand vision, which had been in the making for nearly a decade. In September 2002 President Bush published a new
national security document outlining a set of guiding principles to provide the
anchor for American security over the next fifty years or so.[9] The document
came to be known as the Bush doctrine.

In essence, the foreign policy of George W. Bush had three main elements. First, the United States claimed the right to take unilateral military action to preempt any perceived threat to its security. Second, America declared
its intention to stop the proliferation of weapons of mass destruction. And
third, it would replace hostile regimes with democratic and friendly governments, by force if necessary, in strategically important regions like the Middle
East. The overriding objective was evidently to establish America as the dominant power forever. The document said that "our forces will be strong enough
to dissuade potential adversaries from pursuing a potential military build-up
in hopes of surpassing or equaling the power of the United States."[10]

America is an idealistic country, and its ambition to spread democracy and freedom all over the world is not new. Paul Rogers, a British academic, has described this idealism as coming from a deep-seated conviction that there is only one system, the globalized free economy, set in the context of liberal democracy.[11] George W. Bush took this idealism to a height not witnessed since World War II. He was willing to go to war in one of the world's most volatile regions with the aim of toppling authoritarian regimes America did not like and replacing them with democratic governments. He had a mission to remake the Middle East. Responding to the 9/11 terrorist attacks he bluntly told the world, "you are with us or you are against us" in this war against terrorism.[12]

Whether Bush was an idealist or a realist was a subject of debate by the end of his presidency.[13] In my view, he was unmistakably an idealist throughout.[14] Even in his second term, when he was a lame duck and the Afghanistan and Iraq conflicts were deteriorating, he continued to express confidence that America would prevail.[15] He remained entrenched in his belief in U.S. preeminence, even when events on the ground told a different story and allies were increasingly reluctant to send more troops to fight. Like many idealists, Bush was a captive of his own romantic vision of America as even greater than its undisputed status as the world's only superpower in the twenty-first century.

PAKISTAN

The Taliban militia had emerged, with Pakistan's help, amid the chaos of civil war in Afghanistan two years after the fall of the last pro-Soviet leader, Mohammad Najibullah, in April 1992. Within four years, much of the Afghan territory, including Kabul, was under Taliban control, and the militia had imposed its own brand of Islamic regime on the country. The 9/11 attacks on America changed Pakistan's relationship with the Taliban.

Gen. Pervez Musharraf, Pakistan's military ruler, was one of the first foreign leaders to express shock and outrage at the attacks.[16] In a message to President Bush, Musharraf described terrorism as a threat to the world community. He said that a concerted international effort was needed to fight it in all its forms and manifestations. Musharraf claimed that Pakistan had cooperated in the fight against terrorism in the past and offered his "unstinted cooperation" again. The statement was consistent with the longstanding policy of Pakistan's all-powerful military to present a moderate and secular image of the country in dealing with the United States, no matter what was done nearer home. This had brought great rewards in the form of military and economic assistance in the past and would do so in the future.[17]

It was immediately obvious that Bush and Musharraf were speaking the same language. The U.S. administration was quick to thank Pakistan for its offer of help. U.S. secretary of state Colin Powell announced that the relationship between the United States and Pakistan would develop over time and would stay intact. Powell said America had put a list of specific things before the Pakistani government, which had "agreed to all of those items."[18]

A few days later, General Musharraf told his nation that, after the events of 9/11, America had decided to fight international terrorism and would target Osama bin Laden and the Taliban. He said the Bush administration wanted Pakistan's help in three specific areas: exchange of intelligence, use of air space, and logistic support. Musharraf said that America had support in the UN Security Council and of other Islamic countries. In suggesting this, he implied that there was no other option except to support the Americans. Otherwise, neighbors would try to isolate Pakistan and "our vital interests would be harmed."[19]

General Musharraf called it a critical situation, perhaps "as critical as the events in 1971," when Pakistan's eastern wing seceded, creating an independent country, Bangladesh, with India's help. He evoked the same specter and warned that the country would be in great danger unless it agreed to return to the American fold. While the threat from India was implied, he explicitly mentioned the possibility of an anti-Pakistan government being installed to the west in Afghanistan.

For the Pakistanis, this was a nightmare scenario. In addition to security concerns, the ruling military elite had other worries. Pakistan's economic problems had grown since the decline in American aid after the end of the U.S. proxy war against Soviet and Afghan communism in the early 1980s. There were nuclear weapons, the ultimate deterrent against much larger India, which the military establishment had to safeguard at all cost. America was not pleased about Pakistan's nuclear weapons program. After 9/11, the Pakistani military had to maintain friendly terms with the United States. Otherwise, America or Israel could bomb Pakistan's nuclear installations to eliminate that capacity.

There was also the old Kashmir dispute with India, which the military-political elite of Pakistan had kept alive since independence to maintain national unity. Reminding the Pakistani people from time to time that they needed to listen to their leaders was a powerful psychological tool. General Musharraf thus made sure that the country was willing and ready for a new relationship with the United States.

U.S.-PAKISTAN RELATIONS IN HISTORICAL PERSPECTIVE

Relations between America and Pakistan have been guided by security considerations for both countries since the early 1950s. Pakistan has never been in a situation in which it did not need the United States, but America has been cool toward Pakistan at times. These points came after the demise of the Soviet state, just before the collapse of President Najibullah in Afghanistan, when India and Pakistan fought wars in 1965 and 1971, and when Washington wanted to show its displeasure over Pakistan's nuclear weapons program.[20] When Pakistan's cooperation was needed, America turned a blind eye to the conduct it disapproved of.

Pakistan's security concerns, real and perceived, go back to 1947, when Britain was withdrawing from the subcontinent. I do not intend to go into the causes or history of the partition that led to two separate countries. But it is necessary to record that partition of British India resulted in the creation of a secular, predominantly Hindu India and a Muslim-majority Pakistan. Its two wings, East and West Pakistan, were separated by India. In population, education, industrial infrastructure, and resources, Pakistan was the underdog. Many Indians resented partition on religious grounds and because it allowed a Muslim country to emerge.

Pakistan also fell behind in developing its institutions.[21] There were early setbacks. In September 1948 the country's founder and first governor general, Mohammed Ali Jinnah, died, and Liaquat Ali Khan, the first prime minister, was assassinated in 1951. It was not until 1956, almost a decade after independence, that Pakistan had its first constitution. Barely two years later, it was abrogated following a military coup by General Mohammad Ayub Khan in October 1958. It was the beginning of an era of military authority in Pakistan.

Pakistan's domestic problems and its adversarial relationship with India have had major consequences for the country. Despite Jinnah's desire for Pakistan to be a secular nation for Muslims, the ruling establishment used Islam to control the different tribal and ethnic communities from the beginning and often to suppress demands for autonomy. Internal conflicts and three wars with India gave the military the upper hand.[22] Military intelligence services, especially the Inter-Services Intelligence Directorate (ISI), wielded enormous power in the management of domestic tensions and external relations. ISI took an active role in the determination of defense and foreign policies and has been heavily involved in Afghanistan to give Pakistan influence in that country. This was seen as a necessity to ensure that Pakistan had "strategic depth" across the western frontier in the event of a major Indian attack from the east.

The military's dominant role in government required a large defense budget. In 2007 the total strength of Pakistan's regular armed forces, paramilitary, and coast guard was nearly a million, half of them regular troops.[23] Eighteen percent of the total budget was spent on the military.[24] Secret expenditure on Pakistan's nuclear program and procurement was likely not included in this total. The military in Pakistan has many functions in the formulation of defense and foreign policies and in domestic surveillance, including keeping an eye on Pakistan's bureaucracy, press, and educational system, and it often takes the lead in the maintenance of law and order. Pakistan's armed forces permeate virtually all levels of government and society and have been described as a business.[25]

As this discussion illustrates, America's relationship with Pakistan is based on a direct quid pro quo. America provides billions of dollars in military and economic aid in return for the use of Pakistani territory, facilities, and personnel each time these are needed to meet a U.S. strategic objective. This give-and-take happened at the beginning of the Cold War in the early 1950s, when America fought the Soviet Union in Afghanistan in the 1980s, and again after September 11, 2001.

The emerging threat from the Soviet Union after World War II prompted the U.S.-Pakistan relationship. Only Afghanistan, a remote and poor mountainous country, separated the Soviet Union from Pakistan and the warm waters of the oil-rich Gulf and the Arabian Sea. Pakistan was in crisis, with growing political and economic problems at home and security concerns from India. After a brief period of competition with the USSR for influence in Afghanistan, the Americans settled on forging an alliance with Pakistan, where political and military elites had a Western education or orientation and were easier to do business with. Pakistan was also effective in convincing the administration of President Dwight Eisenhower of its value as a bulwark against Soviet communism. Eisenhower's secretary of state, John Foster Dulles, was at the forefront of Western efforts to build alliances to contain the Soviet Union.

A mutual defense agreement was the start of America's alliance with Pakistan in 1954. Pakistan further aligned itself with the West by joining the U.S.-sponsored South-East Asia Treaty Organization (SEATO) and Central Treaty Organization (CENTO).[26] As a result, the country received about two billion dollars in U.S. assistance, a quarter of it in military aid, until 1961. But America suspended military supplies after the India-Pakistan wars in 1965 and 1971, thereby creating a perception among many Pakistanis that the United States was not a reliable ally.[27]

Military supplies were resumed, only to be stopped again in 1979 by President Jimmy Carter because of Pakistan's secret construction of a uranium enrichment plant in response to India's nuclear test five years before. But the Soviets invaded Afghanistan in December 1979, and the Americans rescinded their decision. The United States again came to view Pakistan as a frontline ally against Soviet expansion. Pakistan had been under military rule since 1977, and Gen. Muhammad Zia-ul-Haq, the military ruler, framed the Soviet action as part of the struggle between communism and Islam. It suited his strategy to isolate and suppress his secular opponents at home and to gain the support of radical Islamist groups.

In 1981 the Reagan administration offered Pakistan an aid package of more than three billion dollars. The military regime, in return, agreed to make the country the main transit point to supply weapons to the Afghan resistance, to recruit and train mujahideen fighters for America's proxy war against the

Soviets, and to gather intelligence. Many of the three million Afghan refugees, from whom anticommunist fighters were recruited, did not return after the fall of communism and played a part in the radicalization of Pakistani society.

The Soviet Union retreated from Afghanistan in 1989, and America again suspended most military and economic assistance to Pakistan as its secret nuclear program became the center of U.S. disapproval. There was considerable resentment over America's refusal to deliver the F-16 fighter planes that Pakistan had bought in 1989.[28] It took nine years for Washington to agree to compensate Pakistan with a cash payment of $325 million and $140 million in goods, including wheat. The episode caused further Pakistani resentment.

The 1990s were a decade of isolation for Pakistan. By then, a clear pattern had been established, with the U.S.-Pakistan relationship fluctuating between high and low points according to circumstances. When Pakistan was needed for America's strategy, it had no choice but to respond to America's call. When the need was no more, Pakistan was isolated and the aid dried up. U.S. assistance helped sustain the ruling military establishment when times were good. Since the armed forces were all powerful, they looked after their own interests in bad times, and the difficulties of the vast majority of Pakistanis became more acute.

RETURN TO THE FOLD AFTER 9/11

When President George W. Bush decided to invade Afghanistan to destroy the Taliban and al Qaeda after 9/11, Pakistan returned to the U.S. fold. The country had been under military rule since a coup by General Musharraf two years before.[29] Musharraf was isolated at home and abroad, and Pakistan had deep economic troubles. Almost a quarter of government revenue came in the form of foreign loans and grants, but servicing on existing debts amounted to nearly half of the government expenditure.[30] Pakistan was forecast to have foreign loans of $21 billion becoming due by 2003, despite having rescheduled nearly $2 billion. Around 40 percent of the population was estimated to be living below the poverty line.

The government of Pakistan was an ally of the Taliban before 9/11. Musharraf's sudden reversal of course—within two days of the attacks—to join the U.S. coalition was an act of a weak state desperate for American support. Musharraf had to abandon the Taliban and soften his stance in support of the insurgents fighting Indian rule in the state of Jammu and Kashmir. Pakistan granted overflight rights to coalition aircraft, allowed U.S. forces to use at least two of its airfields, and agreed to share intelligence.[31] While Pakistan's military regime helped America in capturing some al Qaeda members, others, including its two most senior leaders, Osama bin Laden and Ayman al-Zawahiri, continued to evade arrest because, as was widely suspected, they enjoyed protection inside Pakistani territory.

The concessions General Musharraf had to give to George W. Bush illustrated the Pakistani state's weakness. But its ability to provide sanctuary to the top al Qaeda and Taliban leaders showed that Pakistan's ruling establishment could resist outside pressures when necessary. That Pakistan's military intelligence was not aware of the whereabouts of the most senior al Qaeda and Taliban leaders is inconceivable. However, handing them over to the United States would have been risky. Torture and executions would almost certainly have followed, and there would have been a Muslim backlash at home and abroad, destabilizing Musharraf's own position. There may not have been agreement in the military hierarchy to hand these individuals over to the U.S. authorities, and bin Laden's wealth may have been enough to buy his safety in Pakistan.

THE BUSH LEGACY

As the sole superpower, America during the George W. Bush presidency made many decisions affecting the world, including sending aid to Africa, shifting policy toward India as necessitated by India's emergence as an economic power along with China, and supporting an independent Kosovo. But, in the long run, Bush will be remembered for the war on terror, the consequence of an aggressive, militaristic policy abroad. The war's financial costs were huge. It undermined the role of the United Nations, the well-established international justice system, and the idea of multilateral decision making. Anti-U.S. sentiment was reinforced abroad, not only in the Muslim world but in other parts of the Asian and African continents and in Europe.

It has been said that the Bush administration promoted the war on terror as a new Cold War.[32] There are both similarities and differences between the two. Declarations that the fight against terrorism would be long certainly did much to divide the world into ideological camps. The effects of the rhetoric and actions of each camp at their extreme poisoned the international climate and made the world more dangerous.

There is no denying the inhumanity of 9/11; of the attacks on innocent people in the bombings in Bali, Madrid, and London; and of the language used to justify such acts. But there is also, on the other side, the loss of hundreds of thousands of lives in the bombing of Iraq and Afghanistan, the abuse of detainees at Abu Ghraib prison and the Guantánamo Bay detention camp, the miscarriages of justice, and the apparent eagerness of governments to restrict civil liberties that form the basic foundations of liberal societies. The war on terror brought a climate in which citizens came to suspect fellow citizens and the state assumed extraordinary powers over subjects, including the power to shoot to kill.[33]

Surveillance of citizens without proper judicial authorization and by extralegal means increased, the extent of which was difficult to assess.[34] Governments were still not satisfied and sought to assume greater authority, arguing that many more 9/11-type attacks might happen if they did not have more power. The ideological divide between the authoritarians and the libertarians grew because of entrenched positions, and little effort was made to seek practical solutions to international problems. George W Bush's assertion that he knew for certain that the Guantánamo detainees were "bad people" said it all.[35]

3

BATTLE FOR AFGHANISTAN

It is time for us to win the first war of the twenty-first century.
—George W. Bush, September 16, 2001

The attacks on September 11, 2001, caused a crisis rarely seen in peacetime. One can recall the earthquake in Tangshan, China, in 1976, the Chernobyl nuclear accident ten years later, and the Bhopal gas leak of 1984. These were disasters of major proportions in terms of lives lost and their impact beyond the scene of the events. Chernobyl and Bhopal clearly involved human error or failing, but the attacks on 9/11 were of a different order. Educated men hijacked and crashed passenger aircraft into crowded buildings in an act that was deliberate, callous, and sudden. The consequent shock and horror generated widespread sympathy and support that, although not universal, was overwhelming.

Retaliation by the United States was a foregone conclusion once President George W. Bush had promised to hunt down those directly responsible for the attacks and those who helped them. Mainstream media and governments all over the world condemned the attacks. Middle Eastern countries, including Iran and Libya, were among them. Iraq, however, did not denounce the terrorists' actions. In a barbed reaction, the official newspaper, *Al-Iraq*, described the attacks as "a lesson for all tyrants, oppressors and criminals."[1]

As Palestinian leader Yasir Arafat conveyed his condolences to the Bush administration and the American people, sporadic celebrations of the attacks occurred in the West Bank and some Lebanese refugee camps. Leading Palestinian politician Hanan Ashrawi said the jubilation was a minority reaction, and it would be misleading to focus on it. Even so, the ambivalent nature of popular reaction in the Muslim world demonstrated the gulf between societies there and in the West. The dominance of Israel, seen as an extension of American power, in the Middle East and the Palestinian issue have a lot to do with it. Governments, however, behave in much more calculated ways than people, as dictated by *realpolitik*.

THE MAKING OF A COALITION

The extent of support for America after the events of 9/11 was evident at a meeting of the United Nations Security Council on September 12, 2001. A unanimous UN resolution condemned the attacks, describing them as "a threat to international peace and security." The council expressed its condolences and sympathy to the American people and government and appealed to "all states to work together urgently to bring to justice the perpetrators, organizers and sponsors" of the attacks. The resolution further said that those responsible for supporting or harboring those people would "be held accountable."[2] The General Assembly approved a similar resolution on the same day.[3]

Although the Taliban and al Qaeda denied they had anything to do with the attacks,[4] both expressed approval of what had happened. In a chilling video message, an al Qaeda spokesman, Sulaiman Abu Ghaith, warned there were thousands of young people "eager to die just as the Americans are eager to live."[5] In an interview with the Arabic television network Al Jazeera, Osama bin Laden went further. He was quoted as saying, "We will work to continue this battle . . . until victory or until we meet God before that occurs."[6]

Within hours of the attacks, American investigators had analyzed the hijackers' profiles, and a connection with al Qaeda had emerged. A subsequent British government report cited evidence of a propaganda campaign among like-minded groups of people justifying attacks on Jewish and American targets, bin Laden's assertion before 9/11 that he was preparing a major attack on America, and instructions to close associates of bin Laden's to return to

Afghanistan by September 10, 2001.[7] Indeed, according to the report, some of his associates had named the date of attack as on or around September 11.

The British report concluded that al Qaeda planned and executed the 9/11 attacks. The organization had the will and the resources to launch further attacks of similar scale on the United States and its close allies. Such attacks could not have occurred without the alliance between the Taliban and Osama bin Laden, which enabled bin Laden to enjoy freedom in Afghanistan to promote, plan, and execute terrorist activity.

Tony Blair

Tony Blair was among the most enthusiastic Western leaders to commit Britain to the war on terror. As Bush later acknowledged, the British prime minister was one of the first to call the U.S. president after the attacks, and he visited America on September 20. Blair said that Britain stood side by side with the United States as it had done with Britain in World War II.[8] His language matched that of Bush. The war on terror was "a struggle which concerned all of the democratic, civilized and free world." And Blair said actions had to be taken "to bring to account those responsible" and to dismantle "the apparatus of terror and [eradicate] the evil of mass terrorism in our world" at every single level, in every possible way.

Blair's commitment of total support for George W. Bush at an early stage was portrayed as the continuation of the "special relationship" forged between U.S. president Ronald Reagan and British prime minister Margaret Thatcher in the decisive phase of the Cold War in the 1980s. Although the size and power of their countries could not be compared, the Reagan-Thatcher relationship was between two leaders of comparable stature on the world stage. Staunch anticommunist, free-market ideology played a big part in their relationship, and confronting the Soviet Union was their biggest mission.

Blair had been close to President Bill Clinton when he was in the White House, but it was the events of 9/11 that renewed the talk of the special relationship. Anticommunist ideology had had its day, but the Christian beliefs and almost messianic political mission of both George W. Bush and Tony Blair were the glue that bound them together.[9] Radical Islam was the antithesis that they had to fight. They had to talk up the Islamic threat to demonstrate to themselves, as much as to the international community, that they were fighting a major war to save the "civilized world."

This relationship suited them both. Blair was more articulate, and he traveled widely to make the case for the war on terror. He was extremely popular in America and useful for President Bush to demonstrate that he had international support, particularly when he decided to invade Iraq in 2003. Blair's relationship with Bush gave the prime minister a high-profile role on the world stage, although it also attracted unflattering labels. Some called Blair "Bush's foreign minister" or even "Bush's poodle."

Blair's supporters portrayed him as a statesman using his influence to shape American foreign policy. However, Kendall Myers, a senior analyst at the State Department, reportedly described the relationship as "one-sided," saying that Bush routinely ignored Blair. Myers was quoted as saying that he felt "a little ashamed" at President Bush's treatment of the British prime minister.[10] Blair faced mounting opposition to the war in his own Labour Party and the country and left office in June 2007. He was succeeded by his chancellor of the exchequer, Gordon Brown, who was distinctly less warm to Bush.

Silvio Berlusconi

The Italian prime minister, Silvio Berlusconi, was another high-profile supporter of the war on terror from the beginning. A flamboyant and controversial media magnate, Berlusconi had briefly led a Center-Right coalition government in 1994, when his newly formed party, Forza Italia, entered into separate pacts with the Northern League in northern Italy and the National Alliance in central and southern parts of the country. Berlusconi's government did not survive, but his influence in Italian politics grew steadily, leading to another election victory for his coalition in May 2001.

George W. Bush and Silvio Berlusconi had things in common. Each had a distinctly conservative agenda, with economic policies favoring lower taxes and fewer controls on private enterprise. Bush had had significant business interests before he was elected governor of Texas in 1994. Berlusconi's almost total control of the Italian television network made him the richest man in the country.

Berlusconi had been prime minister of Italy for only a few months before the 9/11 attacks and immediately came out in support of George W. Bush. From then until his defeat in the May 2006 general election, Berlusconi's foreign policy was strongly pro-U.S. Italian troops were deployed to Afghanistan, and, like Tony Blair, Berlusconi supported Bush in his controversial decision to invade Iraq in 2003.[11] Opposition to the war was partly responsible for the narrow defeat of Berlusconi's coalition in the 2006 election.

Although American and British forces led the initial aerial attacks on Afghanistan, Italy deployed its ground troops in 2002, after the Taliban regime had been ousted. Berlusconi's support for Bush appeared more pronounced because it was in marked contrast to the strong opposition to extending the war, and particularly the invasion of Iraq, from France and Germany, two of Italy's closest allies in the European Union.

The war in Iraq was a deeply divisive issue in the European Union, as well as between the EU and George W. Bush throughout his presidency. Italy had about 2,700 troops in southern Iraq—the third-largest foreign contingent after the American and British occupation forces. But these troops were withdrawn from Iraq during the second half of 2006, following Berlusconi's election defeat. In Afghanistan, Italy's military presence continued under NATO command.

Italian governments are notoriously short-lived. After a period of political instability, the governing Center-Left coalition of Prime Minister Romano Prodi collapsed. Italy had another general election in April 2008, and Berlusconi made a return to power for the third time. The circumstances in 2008 were very different, however, with growing concerns over the economy and the Bush presidency in its twilight.

José María Aznar

Prime Minister José María Aznar had led the Center-Right government in Spain for five years before America was attacked on September 11, 2001. Much like Blair, Aznar was a young, popular prime minister who had presided over a period of relative calm in Spain. Both countries were used to secessionist violence—Britain from the Irish Republicans and Spain from the Basque separatists. Like Blair, Aznar pledged Spain's firm support to George W. Bush after 9/11.

America's war on terror had acquired strong momentum by November 2001. And other countries, with their own agendas, had come to join hands with the Bush administration, aware of the need to deal with militancy at home. The Spanish prime minister, too, declared his support for all efforts by America to "track down, to eradicate and to eliminate terrorism wherever it may be worldwide."[12] Aznar promised his cooperation in sharing intelligence and in the deployment of military force in the campaign.

Following the overthrow of the Taliban in December 2001, Spain decided to deploy up to five hundred troops as part of the U.S.-led occupation force in Afghanistan.[13] The size of the contingent was modest, but its significance increased as the Bush administration moved toward a decision to invade Iraq. The Spanish contingent sent to Iraq after the 2003 invasion was around thirteen hundred troops—only about 1 percent of the entire occupation force but the largest contingent from Western Europe after Britain and Italy.

Despite his determined support for President Bush, Aznar was never able to persuade more than a small minority of his own people that war was a good idea.[14] Even so, his conservative Popular Party was ahead in opinion polls until the final stages of the general election campaign in March 2004. Most voters appeared to be satisfied with his Center-Right government, which had presided over an era of economic and political stability, and he was expected to return to power. But then came the Madrid train bombings on March 11, 2004, which killed some two hundred people and wounded fourteen hundred more. Spain's political landscape changed.

In the wake of the death and devastation in Madrid, Aznar and his government claimed that the attacks were the work of the Basque separatists, not al Qaeda. Aznar's motive seemed to be to deflect suggestions that his support for George W. Bush had made Spain a target for groups linked to, or inspired by, al Qaeda. The problem, however, was that the Basque separatists were not known to have the capability to launch such devastating attacks. And police investigations uncovered a van containing detonators linked to the bombing with a recording of verses from the Quran.[15] A dramatic shift in public opinion in Spain occurred just days before the election, and the governing Popular Party managed to snatch defeat from the jaws of victory. The Spanish Socialist

Party won the general election, and Bush lost a staunch ally. Spain promptly withdrew its troops from Iraq.

Even after his defeat Aznar continued to make waves with his uncompromising views. In a speech at the neoconservative Hudson Institute in Washington in September 2006, he said that Muslims should apologize for their eight hundred–year occupation of Spain[16] and described an initiative to encourage dialogue between Muslims and the West as "absurd." The West was under attack and had to defend itself. And, using the language first used by Bush after 9/11, Aznar said, "It is them or it is us. There is no middle ground." He rejected the idea of negotiations with Muslim countries, because they are too radical to deal with.[17]

John Howard

On September 11, 2001, when a hijacked plane crashed into the Pentagon, Australian prime minister John Howard was a short distance away from the scene. The following day, NATO invoked Article 5 of its charter, declaring the attacks on America to be against all nineteen member-states of the alliance. At the same time, Howard, in a conscious decision to join with the Bush administration early in the war on terror, announced that he was invoking the Australia, New Zealand, and United States Security Treaty (ANZUS).[18] In fact, under ANZUS, Australia and the United States had an agreement that called for cooperation only on defense matters in the Pacific Ocean area.

Howard had redefined the provisions of ANZUS in his eagerness to join the war on terror. For, unlike those for NATO member-states, the obligations for ANZUS signatories are vague. Under Article 3, there is little more than a duty to "consult" in the event of a crisis in the Pacific. While the fifty-year-old treaty had been cited before as a reason for tripartite exercises and the presence of electronic surveillance and communication stations, it had never been invoked even when the three nations fought together in Korea and Vietnam.

Australian special forces took part in the early stages of allied operations in Afghanistan, but most of them were withdrawn by December 2002, only to be reinforced later in August–September 2005. At the time of Howard's defeat in the November 2007 general election, the Australian contingent was around a thousand strong. In 2003 he had committed the country to the U.S. decision to invade Iraq, and some two thousand Australian troops were sent to fight in that war. Four years on, the war had become a major issue in the election campaign, and after the defeat of Howard's Liberal Party, Prime Minister Kevin Rudd's incoming Labor government pledged to bring the troops back home. The Australian withdrawal was completed in June 2008.

Just as the Madrid bombing had led to the defeat of a staunch Bush ally, Spanish prime minister Aznar in 2004, Australian opposition to George W. Bush eventually contributed to the fall of John Howard. Memories of the carnage of the October 2002 suicide attack in the Indonesian island of Bali, which killed more than two hundred people, including eighty-eight Australian citizens, and wounded a similar number, kept the Australian participation in the war on terror in the electorate's consciousness. The unpopularity of Australia's involvement in that war finally contributed to Howard's defeat in 2007. The election result ended one of the most enduring political careers in Australian history.[19]

THE INVASION OF AFGHANISTAN

The experience of American casualties in foreign conflicts has shaped U.S. military planning since the war in Vietnam, which ended Lyndon Johnson's presidency in 1968. U.S. administrations in the post-Vietnam era have been well aware of the political cost of American war casualties. In October 1983 241 U.S. servicemen serving in a multinational peacekeeping force in Lebanon were killed in a suicide attack in Beirut.[20] Within four months, President Reagan ordered the withdrawal of the U.S. contingent, and the entire multinational force was removed from Lebanon by April 1984.

Ten years later, on October 3–4, 1993, with Bill Clinton barely settled down in the White House, eighteen American soldiers on a humanitarian mission in Somalia were killed and more than seventy were wounded in an attack by tribesmen linked to al Qaeda. Consequently, U.S. forces were withdrawn from Somalia, and President Clinton became increasingly reluctant to use military intervention in third world conflicts. In 1999 NATO intervened only with aerial bombardment to stop Serbian atrocities against the ethnic

Albanian population in Kosovo, until the Serbian leader, Slobodan Milošević, accepted the conditions for deployment of a peacekeeping force.

The official version of the war in Afghanistan, repeatedly emphasized by the Bush administration, is that the campaign to overthrow the Taliban regime began after 9/11 with heavy air attacks by American and British forces on October 7, 2001. These direct attacks were in contrast to the proxy war in the Afghan theater in the 1980s, when mujahideen fighters were used against the Soviet occupation forces. In the post-Soviet world of the twenty-first century, the Bush administration was overconfident about America's military supremacy and certain that the enemy would be crushed within a short period. So, in the initial phase of the war, America and Britain relied on air and cruise missile attacks, assisted by small special operations units deployed on the ground to gather intelligence and to direct bombing missions to targets. America's infantry was the Northern Alliance, consisting mainly of ethnic Tajik, Uzbek, and Hazara fighters, who had all been squeezed by Taliban advances into little enclaves on the fringes of Afghanistan during the 1990s.

An independent, and quite different, account has emerged from intelligence reports written before September 11, 2001. According to this account, a number of countries—Russia, some Central Asian republics, Iran, and India—helped the opposition Northern Alliance fight against the Taliban regime well before the events of 9/11 and the U.S.-led invasion of Afghanistan.[21] Even more important, George W. Bush had become part of the coalition against the Taliban within weeks of his inauguration as president.[22]

The existence of a coalition of such unlikely partners as the United States and Iran came to light in a report published in *Jane's Intelligence Review* in March 2001. According to *Jane's*, there were regular meetings between America, Russia, and India on ways to strengthen the anti-Taliban forces in Afghanistan. India was providing high-altitude warfare equipment, defense advisers, helicopter technicians, and medics to the Northern Alliance. And the coalition had been operating from bases in the former Soviet republics of Uzbekistan and Tajikistan.

The assassination of the legendary Tajik commander Ahmad Shah Masoud in a suicide attack by al Qaeda two days before 9/11 reinforced foreign support for the opposition forces in Afghanistan. This explains why the

Pakistani military ruler, General Musharraf, suddenly decided to switch support from the Taliban to America's war on terror after the 9/11 attacks. Not doing so would have led to a complete encirclement of Pakistan—something the country's military establishment was determined to preempt.

The first phase of the war on terror in Afghanistan had twin aims: to capture al Qaeda and Taliban leaders and to destroy their organizations. The second phase was to involve the installation of a pro-U.S. government in Kabul in place of the Taliban regime. Survival of the new order would then have to be ensured with long-term support to rebuild the infrastructure and national institutions. Success in the first phase was vital for security, on which everything else depended.

The high-altitude bombing, targeting areas around Kabul, Kandahar, and Jalalabad, continued until the end of October.[23] The object was first to destroy the Taliban's air-defense system and then to hit command, control, and communications facilities. Many of al Qaeda's training camps had been destroyed in the first two weeks, but senior Taliban and al Qaeda leaders had disappeared without trace.

Resistance from al-Qaeda–Taliban forces was strong, despite mounting casualties. An attempt by the Northern Alliance to capture Mazar-i-Sharif in the north was unsuccessful. Two weeks into the campaign, it was clear that using aerial bombardment—designed to minimize American casualties—and Northern Alliance troops was not enough. The Northern Alliance demanded that the air campaign focus more on the front lines separating its troops and Taliban forces.

As the bombing became more intense, civilian casualties began to rise.[24] Thousands of Pashtun militiamen from Pakistan moved into Afghanistan, reinforcing the Taliban against the U.S.-led forces. In this more intensive phase, the Americans used cluster bombs. The pressure on the Taliban appeared to increase suddenly, and the Northern Alliance saw the results it had been hoping for. U.S. special operations troops launched some audacious raids, including one in Kandahar, where a residential compound used by the Taliban leader, Mullah Omar, was targeted. He was not there.

In the bombing campaign of November 2001, up to 90 percent of attacks were directed at supporting the Northern Alliance forces.[25] By the end of November, unmanned aircraft were being used to collect intelligence and attack enemy targets. More special operations units were deployed on the ground to guide allied aircraft. At this point, Taliban and al Qaeda fighters began to melt away from the battlefields.

According to the Israeli intelligence news service DEBKAfile, in mid-November the Northern Alliance was reinforced with two thousand men from the Russian Spetznaz special forces and six thousand men from special Uzbek units, transferred on the orders of President Islam Karimov of Uzbekistan, before a second attempt on Mazar-i-Sharif.[26] These new troops from Russia and Uzbekistan, fighting alongside the Uzbek militia of the Northern Alliance, made a difference. The opposition captured Mazar-i-Sharif, and many Taliban fighters were killed.

Two weeks before the Northern Alliance took the city, President Karimov had rejected a request for help by the visiting U.S. defense secretary, Donald Rumsfeld. Karimov said that he needed his special forces in Uzbekistan to deal with any outbreak of violence at home. He was worried because opposition against the U.S. bombing of Afghanistan was building across the border. However, Russian president Vladimir Putin "persuaded the Uzbek President to change his mind." Putin also informed President Bush that "several dozen Russian agents, together with Uzbek, Kazakh and Mongolian operatives on the payroll of Russian intelligence, had infiltrated Taleban forces."[27]

As opposition forces overran new areas across the country, suspected Taliban supporters were killed in subsequent cleanup operations.[28] One Northern Alliance commander boasted that he had personally executed 160 people. Reports of revenge killings and mounting civilian casualties in U.S. air attacks caused anger in the Muslim world. In one of the strongest attacks, the Iranian supreme leader, Ayatollah Ali Khamenei, said that America was dragging "the world into a war."[29] Aware of the growing resentment among their citizens, even the Pakistani and Saudi authorities criticized the bombing campaign as too long and too intense.

On the war front, the fall of Mazar-i-Sharif and the subsequent brutal revenge killings of Taliban and al Qaeda fighters triggered a chain of events elsewhere. Many of their troops were outflanked and surrounded in the northern city of Kunduz. Even in the south, the Taliban stronghold, the widely feared religious police force was not present in the streets, and on the night of November 12, the regime fled the capital, Kabul.

An early indication that the Bush administration was not prepared for the aftermath of a military victory came with the fall of the Taliban regime. Forces of the Northern Alliance, a coalition of non-Pashtun ethnic groups, were at the gates of the capital. But the Americans asked them not to enter the city for fear of alienating the Pashtuns who had played a dominant role in Afghan society, not only under Taliban rule but also historically.

George W. Bush issued a public warning to the opposition not to seize control of Kabul because "it could endanger hopes for a future broad-based government."[30] Defense Secretary Rumsfeld went further, admitting that America did not have enough forces on the ground to stand in the way of the opposition and that it would be difficult to stop the alliance if it occupied the capital. The Northern Alliance did just that. Its forces entered the capital in defiance of the Bush administration.[31] At the time, Hamid Karzai, a Pashtun Washington had unofficially chosen as Afghanistan's new leader, was in secret negotiations in the south to encourage Pashtun tribal leaders to abandon support for the Taliban.

The history of interventions by imperial powers, namely Britain and Russia, tells us that trying to reshape Afghanistan is perilous. In November 2001 President Bush was determined to reshape Afghanistan, but, as events would show, he did not realize the magnitude of the short- and long-term challenges. The immediate risk was a permanent takeover by the Northern Alliance in Kabul. It would alienate Pashtuns, the dominant ethnic force in Afghan society and Pakistan's frontier areas, and would amount to playing into the Taliban's hands. America was also mindful of the closeness between the Northern Alliance and Russia. While Moscow was part of the coalition against the Taliban, a government with friendly ties to Russia could not be acceptable to the United States and its regional allies, Pakistan and Saudi Arabia.

A Northern Alliance government could also reignite demands for Pashtunistan, a separate homeland for Pashtuns along the Afghan-Pakistan frontier. These demands, seen as a threat to Pakistan's unity, have been strongly resisted by Pakistan's ruling establishment, especially the armed forces. An

Afghan government excluding Pashtuns would have to confront the Pashtun south, and the front lines of the fight would be close to the Afghan capital. There could not be an Afghan government in the post-Taliban period without a Pashtun as its leader.

Nonetheless, the manner in which the Taliban regime collapsed suited the Bush administration. It was achieved without a significant American fighting force on the ground. While Afghan casualties, including civilian casualties, had been considerable, allied casualties had been negligible. Rumsfeld made clear that America had its interests, and the Northern Alliance had its own separate interests. An urgent task for America was to install a friendly government in Kabul, headed by a Pashtun of Washington's choice.

The Bonn agreement of December 2001 was used to appoint Hamid Karzai as chairman of the Afghan Transitional Administration, bypassing the elderly ex-king Zahir Shah, who had been living in exile in Italy since 1973. In January 2002 a traditional assembly, or *loya jirga*, held in Kabul named Karzai president of Afghanistan. A new constitution was approved in December 2003, establishing a presidential system in the country. The first election under the new constitution was held in October 2004, and Karzai was elected to the post.

When the Taliban regime collapsed and melted into the vast, untamed countryside in Afghanistan and Pakistan's frontier, only a small number of U.S. and allied troops were on the ground. According to the U.S. Defense Department, the number rose to about eleven thousand foreign troops, among them five thousand American soldiers, by February 2002.[32] This number was wholly inadequate in a country where a Soviet occupation force of 120,000 had failed to overcome resistance in the 1980s. Afghanistan had lacked a disciplined military and police force since the beginning of communist rule in April 1978. Raising an effective army would be enormously expensive, but security was of paramount importance.

IN AFGHANISTAN, WAR IS PEACE

The United States remains mired in history, exercising power in an
anarchic Hobbesian world where international laws and rules are
unreliable and where true security and the defense and promotion of a
liberal order still depend on the possession and use of military might.

—Robert Kagan

In his essay "Power and Weakness," published in the journal *Policy Review*
in 2002, one of the founders of the Project for the New American Century,
Robert Kagan, contrasted Europe and the United States.[1] Kagan asserted that
Europe was turning away from power into "a self-contained world of laws and
rules and transnational negotiation and cooperation," whereas America preferred coercion rather than persuasion "to seek finality in international affairs."
To see problems solved and threats eliminated, the Americans would use force
and favor unilateralism. They are "less inclined to act through international
institutions" such as the United Nations, "less inclined to work in cooperation
with other nations to pursue common goals," more skeptical about international law, and "more willing to operate outside its strictures" when necessary,
or when "even merely useful."[2]

Few other statements capture the mind-set of many of the leading figures in the Bush administration in its early years. Such a worldview recognizes

no real limitations to what America can do by military means. It expects allies to follow and adversaries to submit to America's will out of fear or after punishment. International law and institutions, many of which the United States created after World War II, do not matter. Acting beyond, or in violation of, the law when it suits the administration's view of the national interest is acceptable. There are no moral, ethical, or legal constraints on the conduct of the world's most powerful nation in this scenario.

As the invasion of Afghanistan was launched, signs of a deficit in America's war strategy began to show. The Bush administration's principal objective was to remove Osama bin Laden and other leaders of al Qaeda and the Taliban and to destroy both organizations, so that never again would there be a terrorist haven in Afghanistan. The United States' dominant position on the world stage—militarily, technologically, and economically—made it a hyperpower. The weaponry it used in the short air campaign to overthrow the Taliban regime was matchless in its sophistication and destructive power. But a country in possession of such a war machine must also have the will to commit itself on the ground.

A military campaign in a theater like Afghanistan requires troops and the capacity to take losses in the battlefield. But the Pentagon had other ideas. It used laser-guided weapons, pilotless drones, and cruise missiles at an unprecedented level. The U.S. military had begun to rely on such technology primarily for two reasons. First, it wanted to avoid suffering a significant number of U.S. casualties, as it had suffered in Vietnam between 1959 and 1975 (58,000 Americans killed and 303,000 wounded) and as the Soviet army had taken in Afghanistan in the 1980s (26,000 Soviet personnel killed).[3] And, second, Defense Secretary Rumsfeld was mesmerized by the idea of employing America's immensely superior technology instead of troops to overwhelm an enemy. The Rumsfeld doctrine was informed by the Vietnam experience. He had been President Gerald Ford's defense secretary in the final days of America's war in Vietnam, when the United States retreated and Communist forces took control of South Vietnam, Cambodia, and Laos.

In November 2001 the dissolution of the Taliban regime under intense bombardment by American and British forces opened the way for the opposition to enter Kabul and towns in the country's north and south. American forces were not there in sufficient numbers to take control of areas evacuated by the Taliban and al Qaeda. From Washington, the Pentagon, with the backing of the White House, continued to pursue the strategy of air attacks, relying on anti-Taliban Afghan militias to fill the vacuum left by retreating forces. Attacks by as many as eighty aircraft and cruise missiles in one day were not unusual.[4]

One of the strongholds of the Taliban and al Qaeda before the U.S.-led invasion was Tora Bora, a network of man-made caves in the White Mountains in eastern Afghanistan, on the edge of Pakistan's autonomous frontier. Tora Bora became a target in the early phase of the air campaign, and the United States started bombing the area on November 16, 2001. Intelligence reports had suggested that Osama bin Laden and Taliban leaders were hiding with hundreds of militants in the caves there.

BAD INVESTMENT IN ISI

Desperately short of paramilitary operatives and local agents, the Central Intelligence Agency was heavily reliant on Pakistan's military intelligence organ, the ISI. The Bush administration had recruited Pakistani president Musharraf in the war on terror two months before the invasion of Afghanistan and was certain that the ISI's loyalty had been secured.[5] But not everyone in the American intelligence community was fooled. Some CIA agents were already worried that the same Pakistani officers who had built up the Taliban were translating reports for American intelligence.

According to intelligence reports that have since been released to the public, a convoy of about a thousand Taliban and al Qaeda fighters escaped to Tora Bora from Jalalabad on November 13, 2001, the same day that Kabul fell to the Northern Alliance. Osama bin Laden was thought to be in the convoy. American planes bombed nearby Jalalabad Airport, but it appears they did not know bin Laden's convoy was moving toward Tora Bora. The Northern Alliance captured Jalalabad the next day. When the bombing of Tora Bora commenced on November 16, the convoy of al Qaeda and Taliban leaders had come and gone.

There were two main routes out of the Tora Bora complex to Pakistan. It turned out that American planes bombed only one route. And more than six hundred Taliban and al Qaeda fighters and many senior leaders escaped via the second route.[6] The much-publicized siege of Tora Bora came too late in December 2001. Pro-U.S. Afghan militia fought only those left behind. Reports from the area said that top al Qaeda leaders had been airlifted by mysterious-looking black helicopters and that al Qaeda was even paying off the pro-American militia to let its operatives escape.

The Tora Bora cave complex was a familiar site for all who were fighting there—including al Qaeda, the Taliban, the ISI, and the CIA. In the early 1980s the original caves were developed and extended with the CIA's help for use by the mujahideen resistance to the Soviet occupation forces. Weapons and ammunition supplied by the CIA were stored there in large quantities as the war against the USSR was prosecuted. It was believed that a large cache of ammunition, including missiles, was left over from that period, and the caves were able to provide a safe haven for as many as a thousand fighters.

While a handful of U.S. soldiers monitored the Battle of Tora Bora and guided bombing missions, they left the actual ground fighting to local forces, hired in haste. The local forces had their own agendas. As a result, America failed in its objective to capture Osama bin Laden and many al Qaeda and Taliban commanders. In a highly critical article, the *Christian Science Monitor* said that the story underlying the Battle of Tora Bora was "how scant intelligence, poorly chosen allies and dubious tactics fumbled a golden opportunity."[7] Michael Scheuer, chief of the CIA's bin Laden desk from 1995 to 1999, said the failure was owing to "the abject fear of American casualties."[8]

Was the flight of senior al Qaeda and Taliban members and hundreds of fighters part of a great escape from Afghanistan to new sanctuaries in Pakistan? Indeed, other cases have been recorded. It is known that, in return for his commitment to America's war on terror, General Musharraf insisted that Pakistani soldiers and ISI personnel fighting with the Taliban or helping them in their battles against the Northern Alliance in Afghanistan be allowed to evacuate.[9] ISI-backed foreign fighters were also evacuated to Pakistan, in part because their capture by the anti-Taliban forces would have compromised the role of Pakistani agencies.

In late November 2001 the imminent fall of the northern Afghan city of Kunduz alarmed the Pakistani military regime. Thousands of Taliban and foreign fighters had retreated to Kunduz from areas seized by the Northern Alliance. Hundreds of Pakistani military officers, ISI advisers, and foreign fighters, including Pakistani volunteers, had been trapped, raising fears of a massacre. Before the city fell to the Northern Alliance on November 25, a series of nighttime flights had evacuated the Pakistanis from there. The reports of the evacuation were vehemently denied at first. But American intelligence and military officers later acknowledged that the Pakistanis were indeed rescued, with the approval of the Bush administration, and an unknown number of Taliban and al Qaeda fighters also escaped.[10]

The recruitment of Pakistan in the war on terror was hasty. The decision was made on 9/11 itself during a telephone conversation between Bush and General Musharraf, and from the outset the partnership suffered from Bush's lack of in-depth knowledge of the sociopolitical conditions of the Pakistani military and the links between the people of Pakistan and Afghanistan. As had several U.S. governments before it, the Bush administration took the simple approach of getting the military ruler of the country most needed on its side, believing that the rest would be easily delivered.

Pakistan is a complex country. Any U.S. military campaign in which lives of Pakistanis, Pashtuns, or Muslims may be lost involves risks that no Pakistani regime can ignore. The Taliban were created by Pakistan and sustained by the ISI until the events of 9/11 forced Musharraf to abandon them in favor of America. Pakistan's pro-Taliban policy had evolved from its security doctrine's twin aims: to defend Pakistan against the Indian threat and to divert the Pakistani Pashtuns from joining their Afghan brethren in reviving the demand for a separate homeland. For influential members of the Pakistani ruling establishment, especially in the ISI, Islam has been a powerful means to control ethnic nationalism. In Pakistan, the desire for a separate Pashtun homeland cannot be bigger than Islam.

Musharraf had to struggle with forces pulling him in opposite directions. On one hand, he had to show loyalty to the Bush administration and be seen to play his part in the hunt for Taliban and al Qaeda operatives. On the other, he had to be sensitive to the support for them in the general population, among Islamist groups, and in the Pakistani military, including the ISI.[11] The Bush administration refused to recognize that Musharraf could not disregard these volatile forces, which had evolved over decades in part as a result of the U.S. campaign to fight the Soviet Union in Afghanistan.

Despite all this, Pakistan could not be totally uncooperative in the war on terror. And the ISI delivered to the Americans several hundred people accused of belonging to the Taliban and al Qaeda, including some high-profile figures.[12] The most prominent was Khalid Sheikh Mohammed, the alleged mastermind of the 9/11 attacks.[13] His arrest, announced in March 2003, came after a long pursuit. He was reported to have fled from a hideout in Karachi following a tip-off in September 2002 but was captured six months later from a Pakistani military officer's "safe house" in Rawalpindi. The officer had family links with the Jamaat-i Islami, an Islamist political party that supported Musharraf.

Sheikh Mohammed, an ethnic Pakistani Baloch born in Kuwait, had been protected and moved around until he was handed over to the United States. There can be little doubt that he was guarded by the ISI. Whether the entire agency was behind the decision to protect him from the Americans is not certain. The ISI is one of the most secretive espionage agencies in the world. What little is known about it does not suggest that the agency's work is compromised by internal divisions. Was the arrest of Khalid Sheikh Mohammed made possible by a deal between Musharraf and the ISI? Or was he handed over to a military officer who was not in the ISI and captured after he was released from the agency's control? The truth has been difficult to establish.

The ISI has been given credit for extending help to the West to frustrate plans to launch terrorist attacks. Pakistani help during the investigations into the 9/11 attacks and the July 7, 2005, bombings in London has been cited as important.[14] However, it is also true that when inquiries appeared to reach too close for comfort, for example to the presence of al Qaeda leaders in Pakistan, the ISI was not so helpful.[15] Other criticisms relate to the ISI's inability or unwillingness to be proactive in sharing its own intelligence with the West, instead of acting on American or British information. There is a strong suspicion that Taliban and al Qaeda leaders, together with Gulbuddin Hekmatyar's Hizb-i-Islami, were allowed to establish themselves in frontier areas, from which they could carry out suicide bombings and other activities.[16] And perhaps thousands of foreign fighters, including Arabs, Chechens, Kazakhs, Tajiks, Uzbeks, and Uighurs, provide them with reinforcements.

RADICALIZATION OF PAKISTAN

The Bush administration's decision to rely on the Pakistani military ruler in the invasion of Afghanistan had looked straightforward immediately after the 9/11 attacks. By the end of 2001 the Taliban regime had been ousted, but the political situation in the region had begun to look much more complex. Under pressure in Afghanistan, the Taliban and al Qaeda found sanctuary in Pakistan's wild territory. General Musharraf did not want the American-led forces to carry out military operations inside Pakistan. America's war on terror in Pakistan had to be prosecuted by the Pakistani military and the costs of all such operations would have to be reimbursed to Pakistan.

Pakistan's military establishment participates in America's wars in the region in a certain way. In the U.S. proxy war against the Soviet occupation forces in Afghanistan in the 1980s, the CIA delivered weapons and money to Pakistan. After that, the ISI controlled which mujahideen groups received the aid and how much.[17] In the war against terror, beginning with the invasion of Afghanistan to overthrow the Taliban from power, the Pakistani military regime insisted on independence in how it carried out operations against Islamist militants inside its territory. In return for logistical support and intelligence cooperation, General Musharraf secured a reversal of American policy. Pakistan became a "major non-NATO ally." Billions of dollars worth of aid, including military hardware, began to flow into Pakistan again. General Musharraf's military regime found respectability on the international stage.

Two considerations drove the foreign policies of most Western countries toward Pakistan in the wake of September 11, 2001: the status of Pakistan as a frontline state in the war on terror and the fear that there would be an Islamist takeover of Pakistan if the military regime were not supported there. Frédéric Grare, an expert on the region, is among those who have challenged these suppositions. He says that the Pakistani military uses the possibility that violent Islamists will throw Pakistan into turmoil and escalate terrorism by seizing power and control of its nuclear weapons "to consolidate its hold on power." The real aim of the military is to manipulate religious political parties and militant groups to achieve its own objectives at home and abroad.[18]

This is a useful starting point for an examination of the radicalization of Pakistani society in recent years. The focus of Grare's analysis is the Islamization of Pakistan. This has been a gradual process, manipulated and hastened by the military regime of Gen. Muhammad Zia-ul-Haq (1977–88),[19] with disastrous consequences. Islamic radicalization continued after Zia's death, during the civilian governments led by Benazir Bhutto and her rival Nawaz Sharif in the 1990s. Bhutto's interior minister, Naseerullah Babar, for example, created the Taliban. Even though religious political parties never did well in elections, and other Islamic organizations were not part of the electoral process, their influence was beyond their support in the country.

The disproportionate influence of Islamic groups in Pakistan is only part of a much wider phenomenon of radicalization, which does not receive the attention it deserves. The role of the military has always been controversial in Pakistan. The use of the army against domestic opposition causes a great deal of resentment among non-Punjabi ethnic communities and in 1971 led to the breakup of the country. Whenever the armed forces seize power, citing the failure of political parties to run the country, military rule aggravates the popular resentment. It leads to a cycle of increasing coercion and protests until the military cannot maintain control from the front. Civilian politicians are then allowed to come forward to provide a facade of legitimacy, until the next army takeover.

The methods of the military, which exercises power directly and from behind the scenes, have contributed to the radicalization of tribal, ethno-nationalist, and secularist forces in Pakistani society.[20] After General Musharraf's ascent to power in the October 1999 coup, Benazir Bhutto and Nawaz Sharif, leaders of the two biggest political parties, were forced into exile. Their parties split. Some of their members switched over to support the military regime, and those who remained steadfast in their opposition were left leaderless.

With martial law in force and national politics in disarray, Musharraf called a referendum, followed by elections, in 2002 to legitimize his regime. The elections allowed an Islamist coalition to rise to power in Balochistan and the North-West Frontier Province (NWFP). The coalition, Muttahida Majlise-Amal (MMA), which favors a theocracy in Pakistan, greatly benefited from the anti-U.S. sentiment generated by Bush's war on terror.

The opposition, including religious parties, became so vociferous that the National Assembly was paralyzed for over a year. In December 2003 General Musharraf reached a deal with the MMA. The pact enabled the pro-Musharraf bloc to raise a two-thirds majority in Parliament, which promptly amended the constitution, retroactively legalizing the 1999 coup by Musharraf and many of his decrees.[21] As a concession, General Musharraf agreed to leave the army by December 2004 because the constitution prohibited anybody from being both president and chief of the Army Staff. He later reneged on the agreement, and his supporters in the National Assembly passed a law that allowed him to remain in both posts.

To many, this was an example of gross abuse of power by the military. The new law led to a major confrontation between Musharraf and the judiciary in 2007. On November 3, as a Supreme Court ruling declaring his incumbency of both posts as unconstitutional looked imminent, General Musharraf declared a state of emergency, suspended the constitution, dismissed the judges, and replaced them with his supporters. Widely described as a second coup, this action gave a new life to the lawyers' movement and radicalized the secular opposition in Pakistan.[22]

The events leading up to the second coup had been extraordinary. Amid growing turbulence, Musharraf was chosen in October 2007 for another presidential term by an electoral college of national and provincial assembly members. Opposition parties either boycotted or abstained, and Musharraf received almost all the votes cast. He finally announced his resignation from the Army Staff and appointed his own successor, Gen. Ashfaq Kayani, though the resignation would not become effective until November. Within weeks of Musharraf's reelection for another five years, the national and provincial legislatures were dissolved to make way for a general election.

Radicalization has also affected the ethno-nationalist and tribal forces in the country. Baloch and Pashtun nationalism, in particular, have mounted strong challenges to the central government since independence in 1947. The main reason for Baloch resentment has been the central government's control over the vast reserves of natural gas, coal, and minerals in Balochistan Province, amounting to about 20 percent of Pakistan's total energy and mineral resources. Despite this, the province has not been economically and socially developed, largely because of "the exclusion of the provincial authorities and local population from decisions on major regional projects."[23]

The inflow of hundreds of thousands of Afghan refugees has changed the ethnic balance in the capital, Quetta, and in the north. Pashtuns are the majority in Quetta and many parts of northern Balochistan. Although Baloch constitute about 60 percent of the province's population, they are mostly scattered in the sparsely populated west, south, and east. Affluent farmers from Sindh have acquired land in the east, increasing pressure on the local population. And many Baloch complain that their province has become a colony of Punjab, the biggest and most powerful province of Pakistan. Gwadar Port, close to the Strait of Hormuz, was built with Chinese capital and labor under the Musharraf regime. China now operates many of the gold and copper mines in Balochistan. The blatant support for Islam and religious parties by the military to counter ethnic nationalism and the arrival of large numbers of Afghan, Arab, and Central Asian militants act like oil in fire.

The effects of the U.S.-Pakistan alliance during Bush's presidency have been devastating for Balochistan. The purpose of American aid was to help the Musharraf regime fight the Taliban and al Qaeda. But, after coming under military pressure in Afghanistan, both organizations moved to Balochistan and the North-West Frontier Province, where they found sanctuary. American weapons were often diverted from even limited operations against al Qaeda and the Taliban toward Pakistan's military campaign to suppress Baloch and Pashtun groups opposed to the central government.[24] In one of the biggest such operations, the eighty-year-old disabled leader of the Bugti tribe, Nawab Akbar Bugti, was assassinated in his mountain hideout. Bugti had a wide following that crossed tribal lines among Baloch groups, and his killing inflamed anti-Musharraf and anti-U.S. feeling.[25]

Radicalization also occurred in Pakistan's North-West Frontier Province, with a rising Pashtun nationalist sentiment in favor of uniting all Pashtuns in northern Balochistan, NWFP, and the Federally Administered Tribal Areas (FATA), a region outside of Pakistan's four provinces that is nominally controlled by the central government.[26] The idea of a greater Pashtun province raises a nightmare scenario for the Pakistani military and intelligence agencies as it would considerably weaken the hold of the central government and of Punjabis in Pakistani politics.

The idea of a greater Pashtun province within Pakistan found support among secular nationalists, led by the Awami National Party. On the other hand, radicalization among Islamist groups took on a more menacing character, bringing the Taliban and Hizb-i-Islami (Hekmatyar faction) together. Pushed by the American-led invasion of Afghanistan, the two most extreme religious groups formed an alliance a decade after Hekmatyar was defeated by the emerging Taliban in the postcommunist phase of the Afghan civil war. This time, though, Hekmatyar was the junior partner, while the Taliban and al Qaeda, their military commands coming ever closer, acquired the dominant role in the growing insurgency.

CHENEY'S SECURITY BUNGLE

When the new occupation powers installed Hamid Karzai as Afghanistan's interim leader in December 2001, strengthening security was the most urgent task before them. The process began with providing the new interim government protection and making Kabul secure. But it was essential to expand the security zone to deprive the defeated Taliban and al Qaeda of space to reestablish sanctuaries. The Bonn agreement was quick to recognize that the new Afghan government was too weak to do the job. So, the agreement called for "the early deployment to Afghanistan of a United Nations mandated force." The UN force was to be expanded from Kabul and surrounding areas to other urban centers and areas beyond.[27]

However, time was of the essence. Many Taliban and al Qaeda leaders had fled with their fighters to Pakistan. Other foot soldiers melted back into their villages. Establishing a security regime in the vacuum was of paramount importance. But in March 2002, Vice President Cheney and Defense Secretary Rumsfeld were already working on the plan to invade Iraq. Cheney publicly rejected the idea of expanding the international peacekeeping force beyond Kabul. America would keep the international force at only the existing level of around five thousand troops. And Cheney made clear that "we are not talking about expanding it to other regions."[28] It was yet another blunder by the Bush administration after the Battle of Tora Bora three months before.

After almost eighteen months, the UN Security Council passed a resolution in October 2003 to allow the expansion of the international force beyond Kabul.[29] But the damage had been done. U.S. reluctance to invest in extending security to far-flung areas undermined President Karzai. Karzai's ability to stand up to warlords and individuals with unappealing pasts was compromised.[30] Although the Bonn agreement sought to accommodate some of the different Afghan factions, Karzai was forced to go beyond—in effect, he had to accept the extremist factions and rely on their private militias to police their own fiefdoms.[31] Karzai tactfully moved some warlords to other positions, but suggestions that he took on the militia commanders' powers are disingenuous.

In 2003 the drug trade was on the rise again, with an estimated value of just over two billion dollars—half the country's gross domestic product.[32] It had risen to four billion dollars by 2007.[33] Private militia commanders in control of the Afghan countryside made large profits from the drug trade at every level, from opium production to processing to export. And these profits went into financing their activities and maintaining their strongholds.

RESURGENT TALIBAN AND AL QAEDA

The period between Cheney's public refusal to commit more troops to expand the security zone in March 2002 and the Security Council resolution allowing further deployment in Afghanistan in October 2003 gave the Taliban and al Qaeda breathing room. They were able to recoup their energy and reestablish themselves along both sides of the Afghanistan-Pakistan border.

Islamic militancy was back in early 2003, months before the Security Council approved further deployment of troops. Recruitment and training of new Taliban militiamen had been going on for several months. Increasingly, mines were being planted, occupation forces were coming under mortar fire, and helicopters were being targeted. By 2007 Kandahar, Kunar, Helmand, Zabul, Paktia, and Khost were the worst-affected Afghan provinces.[34] The Taliban were taking over more and more areas along the Afghan-Pakistan border. Car bombs and suicide attacks had steadily increased.[35] Suicide bombers, in particular, were growing more bold and their attacks were growing more lethal, indicating that al Qaeda was in control of insurgent operations on both sides of the border, while the Taliban provided new recruits.

With security across the border deteriorating, a number of high-profile attacks occurred in both countries. A suicide attack killed the Pakistan People's Party leader and twice prime minister, Benazir Bhutto, in December 2007. Between 2002 and 2008 there were several unsuccessful attempts on the life of President Karzai. On April 27, 2008, insurgents succeeded in penetrating massive security at a military parade in Kabul and attacked an area where dignitaries were sitting. Several people, including a member of the Afghan parliament, died. The Taliban and allies in the Hizb-i Islami said they were responsible.

In 2008 the United States and Britain continued to claim that their military tactics in Afghanistan were succeeding. But the evidence painted a very different picture. As the insurgency persisted, stretching American and NATO forces, units of the newly created Afghan national army and police were deployed in areas infected by the insurgency. And Afghan, instead of foreign, troops began to be targeted. Civilian casualties were many times more, though there is no official count. Savagery on local residents received little media coverage abroad, thereby lending credibility to dubious claims in Washington and London of improvement in security in Afghanistan.

In Pakistan, the conduct of the war became mired in the political struggle between important sections of Pakistani society and the military that dominated the state. Tactical and operational mistakes in the Afghan theater played a significant part in how the situation evolved in both Afghanistan and Pakistan. But perhaps the greatest mistake by the Bush administration was to let the aims of the war against the Taliban and al Qaeda become indistinguishable from the designs of the Pakistani military. And the extension of the war to Iraq ensured the sad neglect of Afghanistan.

As President Bush prepared to leave the White House in January 2009, the gap between claims of improvement in security in Afghanistan and reality grew considerably wider. And Robert Kagan's idea of seeking finality by coercion remained unfulfilled, unless, as George Orwell's *1984* says, war is peace.[36]

5

EXPLAINING THE INVASION OF IRAQ

Good people do not need laws to tell them to act responsibly,
while bad people will find a way around the laws.

—Plato

For more than a year before the invasion of Iraq in March 2003, the United
States, supported by Britain, maintained that Saddam Hussein had a secret
program of weapons of mass destruction. The Bush administration wanted
a regime change in Baghdad and had little patience for the United Nations
weapons inspectors. Their painstaking investigations in the face of Iraqi resistance were slow and did not appear to be heading for the conclusion the
White House wanted.

The decision to invade Iraq will remain the most contentious one President George W. Bush made. The war is an event that will affect a whole generation, and perhaps several generations. Whether it was the beginning of an
experiment in democracy in the Middle East or an attempt to secure the oil
supply for the United States, one thing is certain: the decision to go to war
was not based on Iraq's weapons of mass destruction, as claimed in a British
dossier on Iraq.

A year before the U.S.-led invasion of Iraq, British prime minister Tony
Blair told the Bush administration that Britain backed regime change, but

the plan had to be clever. The British ambassador to Washington, Christopher Meyer, wrote to the Prime Minister's Office in London about a meeting he had had with Deputy Secretary of Defense Paul Wolfowitz on March 17, 2002:

> It would be a tough sell for us domestically, and probably tougher else-where in Europe. The US could go it alone if it wanted to. But if it wanted to act with partners, there had to be a strategy for building sup-port for military action against Saddam. I then went through the need to wrongfoot Saddam on the inspectors and the UN Security Council resolutions and the Middle East peace process as an integral part of the anti-Saddam strategy.... I said that the UK was giving serious thought to publishing a paper that would make a case against Saddam. If the UK were to join the US in any operation against Saddam, we would have to be able to take a critical mass of parliamentary and public opin-ion with us.[1]

If a case against Saddam did not exist, it would have to be invented. The Security Council had entrusted the UN weapons inspection team to investi-gate the Iraqi weapons program. In November 2002, under mounting pres-sure, Iraq had agreed to cooperate with the UN inspection regime for the first time since December 1998, when inspectors had been withdrawn.[2] For eight years before 1998, inspectors had conducted searches and destroyed materials considered illegal under the UN regime. But their work had also experienced a few crises. The Iraqi regime was predictably difficult with the inspectors, accusing them of spying for the Central Intelligence Agency so that America could use the information to attack Iraq in the future. In August 1998 the American inspector Scott Ritter resigned from the UN team. Ritter accused the Clinton administration of contributing to Saddam's defiance and Ameri-can intelligence services of conducting their own operations in the guise of providing information to the UN inspectors.[3] An ex-U.S. Marine Corps of-ficer himself, Ritter later became a critic of the Bush administration's plan to invade Iraq. In an interview on the BBC program *HARDtalk* on October 6, 2003, he told David Jessel that the United Nations had accounted for between 90 and 95 percent of Iraq's WMD capability during its work.

After the resumption of inspections in November 2002, the head of the UN Inspection Commission, Swedish diplomat Hans Blix, gave periodic reports to the Security Council. At first the inspectors encountered difficulties, but the job became easier with time. The number of Iraqi agents monitoring and restricting the work was reduced from five to one per inspector. The UN team was able to cast its net wider, checking industrial sites, ammunition depots, research centers, universities, even presidential sites. On February 14, 2003, Blix told the Security Council that, of the chemical and biological samples the team had collected so far, three-fourths had been analyzed. All of the results had been consistent with Iraqi declarations. How much, if any, was left of Iraq's weapons of mass destruction program? Blix said the UN team had not found anything. And he expected Iraq to continue to comply with the inspection regime.

The idea of invading Iraq was much more contentious outside America than the invasion of Afghanistan had been in 2001. Because al Qaeda had launched the 9/11 attacks and the Taliban regime had given it sanctuary in Afghanistan, the United States was allowed recourse, and the case for action to prevent further attacks was strong. Iraq was, however, a different matter. The Bush administration argued that Saddam Hussein, a brutal and an unpredictable dictator, had to be contained. Many doubters argued that the containment of his regime was progressing and the removal of the Taliban from power in Afghanistan would add to the pressure on him. Saddam may have come to realize that the West meant business, and his compliance with the UN inspection regime, as reported by Blix, was indicative of such recognition. On March 7, 2003, less than two weeks before the invasion, Blix informed the Security Council that Baghdad had tried to persuade the UN team that Al Samoud II missiles, which it had already declared, fell "within the permissible range" set by the council. However, a panel of international experts had reached the opposite conclusion. Blix said the Iraqi regime had subsequently agreed to destroy the missiles and related items, and the process of destruction had begun under UN supervision.

As far back as 1878–79, German philosopher Friedrich Nietzsche gave the world an aphorism of timeless relevance: "Convictions are more dangerous enemies of truth than lies." In the case of Iraq, George W. Bush and Tony Blair were blinded by their convictions, which left no room for conflicting views and stifled the search for truth. They were certain that the world would be a better place without Saddam and simply needed to build support for military action to overthrow him. This support would come in the form of a British dossier on Iraq, published on September 24, 2002, claiming that Saddam Hussein had usable chemical and biological weapons capability, which included "recent production of chemical and biological agents." He had shells, bombs, sprayers, and ballistic missiles to deliver these weapons. And the Iraqi military was "able to deploy [them] within 45 minutes of a decision to do so."[4]

Blix's progress reports for the Security Council flew directly in the face of the British dossier on Iraq. Bush and Blair were outraged but remained adamant that their intelligence was accurate. As a U.S.-led attack became imminent and President Bush warned all foreigners to leave Iraq, the UN inspectors were withdrawn. The invasion went ahead, beginning with Operation Shock and Awe, which included massive aerial bombardment, as well as ground missions by special operations forces.

The UN's role in Iraq had ended. Blix left his post and became an outspoken critic of the invasion of Iraq, which he described as illegal.[5] The U.S. and British position was further undermined when United Nations Secretary General Kofi Annan said in a BBC World Service interview in September 2004 that "the invasion of Iraq was an illegal act that contravened the UN Charter."[6]

ARMING IRAQ IN THE 1980S

The failure of the United States and its allies to find WMDs in Iraq undermined the case for the 2003 invasion. But Saddam Hussein did use chemical weapons in the 1980s, when Iraq fought against Iran, and the West helped Saddam Hussein. The strange relationship between Iraq and the West reminds one of an observation Niccolo Machiavelli made five centuries ago. Machiavelli saw politics as having "no relation to morals." Iraq was also a close ally of the Soviet Union, and the Ba'athist regime in Baghdad was steeped in socialist ideology. The last and fiercest phase of the Cold War was being fought in Afghanistan while Iraq was at war with Iran. And yet the United States, under President Reagan, was collaborating with Iraq.

Saddam Hussein had invaded Iran in September 1980, in a disastrous miscalculation that the Islamist regime, which had overthrown the pro-U.S. shah of Iran, would be too weak to stand up to the Iraqi military. It turned out to be one of the longest conflicts of the twentieth century, with no victor emerging when the war ended eight years later. America first waited to see a collapse of the Iranian regime under internal and external pressures. Contrary to the initial expectation, Iranian troops in the summer of 1982 had advanced to within a few miles of Basra, Iraq's second-largest city. Washington feared that the entire region, including Saudi Arabia and Kuwait, would be destabilized, threatening oil supplies. Thus the Reagan administration backed Iraq, which was removed from the State Department's list of known terrorist countries in February 1982, despite strong objections from Congress.[7] In 1983 the Reagan administration approved the sale of sixty Hughes helicopters to Iraq, supposedly for "civilian use," although they could be equipped with weapons within hours. And, as Patrick Tyler wrote in the *New York Times* on August 18, 2002, the Defense Intelligence Agency, between 1982 and 1988, provided Baghdad with detailed information on Iranian deployments, tactical battle plans, maps for air attacks, and damage assessments.[8]

The U.S. tilt toward Iraq was formalized in policy in November 1983 amid severe anxiety in Washington that the Iraqi state might collapse. Even though Saddam Hussein's gamble in attacking Iran had backfired, America's fears of Iraq's imminent fall were probably exaggerated because Washington had underestimated the power of Iraqi nationalism as it had underestimated Iranian nationalism in the 1970s. It was known at the highest levels in the Reagan administration that the Iraqi troops were using chemical weapons against the Iranians. But the United States had committed itself to the Saddam Hussein regime. His chemical weapons took a backseat. In December 1983 Reagan's special envoy to the Middle East, Donald Rumsfeld, was sent to Baghdad, where he met Saddam and Tariq Aziz, his foreign minister.[9]

A sworn affidavit by Howard Teicher, an official who worked for the National Security Council at the time, reveals previously unknown information about the means by which America supplied weapons to Saddam Hussein in the 1980s. According to the affidavit, CIA Director William Casey and his deputy Robert Gates thought that Iraq needed cluster bombs and antiarmor weapons to stop "human waves" of Iranian troops. Both Casey and Gates "knew of, approved of, and assisted in the sale of non-US origin weapons, ammunition and vehicles to Iraq." America had non-U.S. weapons in large quantities—mainly of Soviet design—and could have more manufactured. When specific items, such as antiarmor weapons, could not be secured from non-U.S. suppliers, American weapons were sent to Iraq.[10]

The CIA had a program called Bear Spares, under which Soviet-style weaponry, seized in the previous Middle East conflicts or manufactured, was sent to the Iraqi regime. This program was developed a short time after Israel had bombed the French-built Osirak nuclear reactor near Baghdad. The government of Menachem Begin said it believed the plant was designed to build nuclear weapons for use against Israel. If Saddam had succeeded in designing such weapons, Iraq would have acquired atomic weapons the size of that dropped on Hiroshima. Israel said it would never allow such nuclear development and criticized both France and Italy for supplying Iraq with nuclear materials. Yet, Teicher says in his sworn affidavit that in 1984 Rumsfeld offered Aziz military assistance that could be sent to Iraq via Israel. Aziz firmly rejected the offer, saying that he would be executed on the spot if Saddam ever learned that he had accepted Israeli aid.[11]

The main thrust of Rumsfeld's message during his visits to Baghdad in the 1980s was that the Iraqi regime had broad latitude in prosecuting the war against Iran. Saddam Hussein had clearly built up his arsenal of chemical weapons, including poison gas. In 1982, for example, the Iraqi army employed riot control agents to repel Iranian advances. It had begun resorting to the use of mustard gas by mid-1983, and in March 1984 it employed tabun in the first ever use of a nerve agent in war.[12] The Iraqis continued using chemical weapons until the end of the war in 1988. They had by then progressed to the use of sarin, which disrupts the nervous system and ultimately suffocates its victims. Mustard gas and nerve agents were also used between 1983 and 1988 to attack Iraqi Kurds opposed to Saddam—and against Shi'a rebellions in the early 1990s, after Iraq's defeat in the first Gulf War.

All of these attacks—against Iranian troops and against Iraqis—happened under America's watch, even after the 1991 Gulf War, when air-exclusion zones had been imposed over the Kurdish north and the Shi'a south of Iraq.[13]

Western aircraft flying in these zones watched thousands of Iraqis suffer from being gassed, without taking any action to stop Saddam. The world did not have any illusions about the brutal dictator. The "civilized" West—America in particular—suffered an indescribable loss of moral authority and credibility. Coming immediately after the war to liberate Kuwait from Iraqi occupation, the attacks shattered illusions that America was in the region to protect human life and the principles of liberty and dignity.

After the invasion of Iraq in early 2003 and months of searches, the chief of the Iraq Survey Group, David Kay, said in his October 2003 report that no weapons of mass destruction had been found in Iraq.[14] Kay's report contradicted pre-war claims by the Bush and Blair administrations about the imminent threat from Iraq's chemical and biological weapons. But such weapons had been used in the 1980s and early 1990s. So, where did they go?

The answer came in the transcript of a discussion in August 1995 between UN weapons inspectors and a high-ranking Iraqi defector, Gen. Hussein Kamal, former weapons chief in Saddam's regime and the dictator's son-in-law. Kamal had taken thousands of documents about Iraq's weapons of mass destruction program out of the country with him. Talking about the 1991 Gulf War, Kamal told the UN inspectors that Saddam had feared a massive U.S. retaliation if chemical or biological weapons were used against coalition troops: "They realized that if chemical weapons were used, retaliation would be nuclear. . . . I ordered the destruction of all chemical weapons. All weapons—chemical, biological, missile, nuclear were destroyed."[15]

The American and British diplomatic offensive to counter opponents and doubters of the impending invasion of Iraq was ceaseless to the end. Six weeks before the bombing of Iraq began, Secretary of State Colin Powell gave a dramatic presentation at a UN Security Council meeting. He claimed that Saddam had weapons of mass destruction that threatened not only the Middle East but also the rest of the world. A key part of Powell's case, about biological weapons, was based on information provided by a single Iraqi agent, code-named Curveball.

In November 2007 a small number of documents obtained by the National Security Archive about the information provided by Curveball were published.[16] They showed that the agent code-named Curveball, Rafid Ahmed

Alwan, had deceived Western intelligence several times, first in Germany, where he appeared in a refugee camp in 1999. The CIA had serious doubts about Alwan, who was later described on the CBS investigative news program *60 Minutes* as "a liar . . . a thief."[17] Although these doubts were relayed to Powell, his presentation in the Security Council remained unaffected. It confirmed the Bush administration's determination not to let facts get in the way of its plan to invade Iraq. The United States has the most sophisticated military technology in the world. Its spy planes and satellites regularly photograph the globe, including both adversarial and friendly countries. The notion that the Bush administration needed a single Iraqi informer, whose credibility was suspect, to decide to invade the country is absurd.

WAR WITHOUT A CLUE

Winston Churchill said that "a fanatic is one who can't change his mind and won't change the subject." The mind-set of a fanatic is resistant to advice and rational or moral persuasion. America's shock and anger after the 9/11 attacks were natural. The Bush administration's determination to identify the attack's origins and to act was understandable. However, by the time the invasion of Iraq came in March 2003, the rationale had begun to lose its meaning.[18] The lives of innocent men, women, and children in Afghanistan, Iraq, and elsewhere did not matter to the Bush administration. The occupation powers in Afghanistan and Iraq did not even bother to count casualties of the war on terror.[19] The religious fanaticism of al Qaeda was responsible for the carnage at the World Trade Center and the Pentagon. Equally, the messianic zealotry in Washington and London must take responsibility for the decision to invade Iraq, the miscalculations at the time, and what has happened since in the name of fighting terrorism.

On March 19, as zero hour approached, the U.S.-led coalition had plans to begin the invasion with a spectacular "decapitation" strike targeting the most senior fifty-five men in the Iraqi leadership. However, a tip to the CIA intervened. The agency had learned that Saddam Hussein would be at a certain place at the scheduled time of the attack, and the original plan was abandoned. Instead, cruise missiles and stealth bombers raided the Dora Farms complex in southeastern Baghdad. Unfortunately the intelligence had been wrong, and Saddam was not there.[20] The Americans had assumed that he would be hiding in some underground tunnel and opted to use "bunker-buster" bombs. In fact, the compound had no tunnels, and the missiles aimed at the central palace missed the target.

A massive bombardment of Baghdad and other Iraqi cities began within two days of the failed operation. CNN and CBS reported how tremendous explosions rocked the Iraqi capital, hitting targets that were supposedly chosen with precision. So certain were the architects of the war that they named the operation Shock and Awe. More than sixteen hundred missions, one-third of them using cruise missiles, were unleashed in the next forty-eight hours. Rumsfeld echoed what Pentagon military officers claimed was the operation's aim: "To instill shock and awe in the Iraqi regime and to convey to Iraqis that Saddam and his leadership were finished."[21]

The bombing was not as precise as the Pentagon claimed. Thousands of civilians, perhaps many more, were killed, and property and infrastructure were destroyed in the immediate blitz. It might have been a marvel for war reporters and some of those watching television news in their living rooms in the United States and Europe. For the Iraqi population, it was anything but that. An article on March 24, 2003, in Britain's *Guardian* newspaper made the point that nobody in Washington seemed to have anticipated Shock and Awe's impact in the wider world. The author of the article, Brian Whitaker, wrote, "To some in the Arab and Muslim countries, Shock and Awe is terrorism by another name; to others, a crime that compares unfavorably with September 11." Whitaker was struck by scenes on television of middle-class Americans singing patriotic songs around their dinner tables, as Shock and Awe decapitated the Iraqi state, infrastructure, and society.

One of Washington's key assumptions before the war was that, as the ground invasion began in southern Iraq, American troops would be greeted by the Shi'a population that had suffered much under Saddam. The Bush administration further thought that U.S. troops would not have to fight in the south, so there would be no need to secure the region. They would swiftly march to Baghdad, where the fiercely loyal Republican Guard would likely mount a serious challenge and where the real battle would be fought.

As it turned out, there was a lot of opposition in the southern cities from guerrilla fighters, who surprised the coalition forces and slowed their advance toward the capital. The battles for Nasiriyyah, the fourth-largest Iraqi city; Najaf, one of the holiest places of Shi'a Islam; and Basra were fierce. While Saddam's impending demise was good news for the Iraqi Shi'a community, its attitude to the United States was influenced by at least two major factors: first, America's failure to intervene to stop Saddam's brutal suppression of the Shi'a uprisings in the south in 1991, and second, a strong pro-Iranian and therefore anti-U.S. sentiment throughout the Iraqi Shi'a community. The Bush administration did not realize that the Shi'a of Iraq had no reason to readily collaborate with the United States after more than two decades of hostility between Tehran and Washington.

Power fills emptiness like air and water. When a state disintegrates, the calamity leaves a vacuum that cannot remain. New players, internal and external, emerge to take the place of the institutions that had hitherto kept order in society. History has taught humankind this lesson through centuries, at its worst within living memory in Afghanistan, Lebanon, Somalia, and Yugoslavia. These conflicts were enough to remind the architects of the war on terror of the risks in Iraq. Nietzsche gave a warning more than a century ago that remains relevant today: humans should be careful while fighting monsters not to create new ones.

America's failure to kill Saddam on the first day of the attack owing to wrong intelligence made the bombing of Iraq more vicious. There were some battles with units that were especially loyal to Saddam: the Republican Guard and Fedayeen Saddam paramilitary troops. But under the increasing pressure of aerial bombardment, advancing ground forces, and CIA leaflets dropped from air telling Iraqi soldiers to go home and await further instructions, the bulk of the Iraqi armed forces melted away. Soldiers simply went home with their weapons instead of offering significant resistance to the invading forces. In his account of the capture of Baghdad, *New York Times* correspondent Todd Purdum told PBS *Frontline* on January 29, 2004, that Saddam was expected to preserve his military strength to defend the capital, but the resistance was far less than anticipated. The Americans viewed it as an indication that the Iraqi military had rapidly crumbled. On April 9, as Saddam's statue was pulled down at Baghdad's Firdos Square, there was a sense of triumph in Washington. President Bush expressed his undiluted delight that the statue had come down, and in the Pentagon, Donald Rumsfeld compared the apparent success of the war to the fall of Hitler, Lenin, Stalin, and all other regimes of repression around the world.

As Iraq fell to the U.S.-led coalition, the Bush administration appointed Jay Garner, a retired U.S. Army lieutenant general, as head of the Office of Reconstruction and Humanitarian Assistance in Iraq. Garner had been popular in a similar role in the Kurdish-populated Iraqi north. His ideas were radically different from the neoconservatives, who were by then in total control of Iraq policy. His plan would never have found favor in Washington. He wanted to hold elections in Iraq within ninety days, to pull American troops out of cities and retreat to desert bases, and to have the new Iraqi government decide how to run the country and what to do with its assets. As Greg Palast, an award-winning journalist and documentary filmmaker, says on his website, seizing title and ownership of Iraq's oil fields was not on Garner's must-do list. Palast quotes Garner as saying, "It's their country . . . their oil."[22] Garner was quickly replaced by Paul Bremer in early May 2003. As head of the Coalition Provisional Authority—in effect the governor of Iraq—Bremer acquired total control over the fallen country and reported directly to Defense Secretary Rumsfeld.

Two early decisions are widely seen as the trigger that unleashed a war of all against all in Iraq. With order number 1, issued on May 16, 2003, Bremer dissolved the Ba'ath Party. With it collapsed the state structure—both the military and the civil service—which employed large numbers of Iraqis to run the country. In an article in *Le Monde Diplomatique*, Toby Dodge, a British scholar, described the Iraqi population a month after the arrival of the U.S. forces as dominated by a Hobbesian nightmare.[23] He estimated that between 20,000 and 120,000 senior and middle-ranking employees lost their jobs in the civil service purge. They would have constituted the very force to be used to restore order amid violence and looting—for seventeen of Baghdad's twenty-three ministries were completely gutted, stripped first of all portable items, such as computers, and then of furniture and fittings—all within three weeks. There were not enough U.S. troops to stop it.

In a subsequent move, Bremer issued order number 2, which formally dissolved the most important state institutions and their subordinates, such as government ministries, Iraqi military and paramilitary organizations, the National Assembly, courts, and emergency forces. Preparing alternatives to take over the functions of these organizations in a country of 30 million people was essential. But the two edicts, with no alternatives in place, were a triumph of vindictiveness over rationalism. They caused the complete collapse of the Iraqi state's administrative and coercive capacity, leaving a vacuum that was rapidly filled by new violent players.

After the invasion, Iraq became a theater not only of America's war on terror but also of a number of simultaneous, overlapping conflicts. Rival forces turned on each other and left millions of innocent victims in the country. As the Iraqi armed forces disintegrated and their entity was formally dissolved by orders number 1 and 2, violent criminal gangs rose in the cities. After looting public assets, they turned against Iraq's middle class, terrorizing, killing, and plundering ordinary citizens. U.S. troops were neither sufficient in numbers nor did they have the will to prevent the reign of lawlessness.

The period of euphoria over the fall of Saddam Hussein was short. In addition to crime, armed opposition to the occupation of Iraq, composed of Islamist and Iraqi nationalist groups with as many as fifty thousand insurgents in their ranks, soon built up. Al Qaeda, which was not a force in Iraq until the invasion in March 2003, moved in, as it came under more pressure in Afghanistan. Al Qaeda was thought to have been behind the bombing of Al-Askari Mosque in the Iraqi city of Samarra, one of the holiest shrines of Shi'a Islam, in February 2006, and the country was soon in the grip of full-scale civil war. Shi'a versus Sunni, pro- and anti-U.S. forces, supporters and opponents of Iran and Saudi Arabia, Shi'a against Shi'a, and Sunni against Sunni—all these and more players sank into a conflict that had its roots in centuries of resentment against foreign powers and that exploded because of the complete failure of George W. Bush and Tony Blair to understand Iraqi society.[24]

HUMAN RIGHTS IN ACUTE CRISIS

Powerful governments and armed groups are deliberately
fomenting fear to erode human rights and to create an
increasingly polarized and dangerous world.
—Amnesty International, May 23, 2007

On the day Amnesty International published its 2007 human rights assessment worldwide, its message reflected something that had become increasingly obvious. The war on terror had left a long trail of human rights abuses
and created deep divisions that cast a shadow on international relations, making the world more dangerous. In one of the strongest repudiations of Western government policies, Amnesty's secretary general, Irene Khan, said, "The
politics of fear is fuelling a downward spiral of human rights abuses in which
no right is sacrosanct and no person safe." She accused the West of adopting
policies that undermined the rule of law, fed racism and xenophobia, divided
communities, intensified inequalities, and sowed the seeds for more violence
and conflict.[1] Amnesty said that old-fashioned repression had gained new life
under the guise of fighting terrorism in some countries, while in others, including the United Kingdom, loosely defined counterterrorism laws posed a
threat to free speech.

Among leaders who were cited for playing on fear among their supporters to help them push their own political agendas and strengthen their political

power were President George W. Bush, Prime Minister John Howard, President Omar al-Bashir of Sudan, and President Robert Mugabe of Zimbabwe. When leaders of the free world find themselves in the same league as the most barbaric dictators when it comes to human rights, there is a serious problem.

The 2008 Human Rights Watch report mourned the state of democracy: "Rarely has democracy been so acclaimed, yet so breached, so promoted yet so disrespected, so important yet so disappointing."[2] From Pakistan, China, and Russia to Uzbekistan, Egypt, Ethiopia, and Zimbabwe, every dictator or totalitarian regime aspires to the status conferred by the label of democracy. The rhetoric that President Bush introduced at the beginning of his war on terror and crusade for democracy gave such regimes new life as they claimed legitimacy for their coercive behavior against their own citizens in the name of fighting terrorism and as partners of the free world. Human Rights Watch accused the Bush administration of embracing the route of the dictator instead of defending human rights. These days discussions of human rights inevitably fall on the Guantánamo Bay detention camp, secret CIA prisons abroad, waterboarding and other forms of torture, military commissions, and the suspension of habeas corpus.[3] Amnesty International and Human Rights Watch are two of the world's leading organizations in the field of human rights. How did they reach conclusions so bleak?

The dawn of the twenty-first century bears a strange resemblance to the era that led to the grant of Magna Carta in 1215. In the early thirteenth century, King John of England invaded France and, in the ensuing wars, captured significant territory in the west. By 1214, though, he had overstretched his military, and that year he was defeated in the Battle of Bouvines, near Lille. Overall the wars were disastrous, and the costs in lives and money were unsustainable. Moreover, the king lost income that the territory in France had generated. He demanded higher payments from his barons to make up for the deficit and more men to serve as knights in his military. The king did not have much sympathy for his subjects. He appointed all of England's county judges, who imposed harsh penalties on dissenters, seizing their properties and possessions in many cases.

In 1215 King John was deeply unpopular. His policy of fighting ruinous wars and funding them through excessive coercion against his own subjects generated resentment. At a time of economic difficulties, his efforts to raise money and troops caused extreme hardship for the people in his kingdom. When taxes were not enough, people, including women and minors, were sold. Some of the most important barons complained that the king's demands had become unreasonable and rebelled. They were supported by the city of London and others who did not openly revolt.

King John's authority had already suffered because of a bitter dispute with the pope over the appointment of the archbishop of Canterbury. The pope ultimately appointed Stephen Langton against King John's will,[4] and he excommunicated the king and took over his kingdom as a feudal fief. These setbacks did not stop John from launching a crusade to recapture the Holy Land from the infidel Muslims in early 1215. This continued overextension further contributed to the barons' grievances, and their rebellion posed a grave threat to his crown.

In an attempt to avoid a civil war, King John put his seal on two documents of concessions in June 1215. One was Magna Carta, the Great Charter of Freedoms. The other, the Charter of the Forest, granted subsistence rights to the poor. Magna Carta was not a bill of rights for the king's subjects, but an armistice, on which he swiftly reneged, resuming war on the barons and conspiring with the pope against them. In revenge, the barons invited Louis of France to invade England in May 1216. In October John was dead, and Magna Carta was saved by the French invasion. Under the treaty of peace on September 11, 1217, Louis renounced any claim to the English throne, and the two charters of liberties were restored.[5]

Many ideas in Magna Carta have been repealed or amended through centuries, but other principles remain the source of the most fundamental freedoms today—for every individual. The right of habeas corpus, prohibition of torture, trial by jury, and the rule of law—all derive from Chapter 39 of the Great Charter of 1215, which says that no free man shall be arrested, imprisoned, victimized, or attacked in any way, except by the judgment of his peers or by the law of the land. Habeas corpus is an extraordinary legal remedy. It empowers courts, and even places a duty upon them, to command the state to produce a person whose liberty has been taken away and show cause why. It is the ultimate safeguard against unlawful detention and is written in the U.S. Constitution, English law, and all of Magna Carta's derivatives throughout the world.

Today legal experts use the adage "Justice delayed is justice denied."[6] Every individual has the right to be produced in court without delay and to have a speedy trial once charged. Delaying trial is unfair to the injured party, who must be presumed innocent until proven guilty. This promise can be traced back to Chapter 40 of Magna Carta, which states, "To no one will we sell, to no one deny or delay right or justice."

The Fifth Amendment of the U.S. Constitution grants due process of law and requires formal accusation by a grand jury in order for one to be imprisoned for a criminal offense. It says that no one shall be forced to be a witness against him or herself; deprived of life, liberty, or property; or tried twice for the same offense. Furthermore, the Fourteenth Amendment, ratified in 1868, following the Civil War, refers to due process and notably to "equal protection of the laws." Originally, it was intended to secure rights for former slaves just after the abolition of slavery. It is now the foundation for American ideals of fairness and justice. These ideals have been further preserved in international law written since the end of World War II.

Yet despite these laws, human rights have continued to be violated in the second half of the twentieth century. The offenders were mainly the Soviet Union, China, and states that were portrayed as having been aided and abetted by the communists. The West itself sustained unpleasant regimes in the name of fighting communism, but on the whole, the United States and its allies occupied high moral ground. Totalitarian regimes were rightly condemned, and millions of refugees were given asylum in the West. The fall of the Berlin Wall in 1989 started a rapid collapse of the Soviet empire, and within two years the USSR was dissolved. There was widespread ecstasy. Yet, ten years later, the Gulag system that had given the Soviet Union such a bad name was reborn—this time as a creation of the United States.[7]

On September 6, 2006, President George W. Bush admitted the existence of a secret CIA program to abduct, detain, and interrogate people outside of America as part of his war on terror. In a carefully worded statement, intended to portray himself as a strong leader, Bush referred to the CIA interrogation techniques as tough, lawful, and necessary: "We are getting vital information necessary to do our jobs and that is to protect the American people and our allies."[8] The president said he could not describe the methods used in the CIA program. He said he wanted everyone to understand why. The admission followed months of media reports in America and Europe and protests by nongovernmental organizations that made the administration's continued silence untenable.

Why had the U.S. administration chosen to operate these prisons abroad? Where were they located, and what kind of interrogation techniques were used to obtain the "vital information"? Glossy assertions, made under the pretense of confidentiality, became the hallmark of the Bush administration as the war on terror progressed. We in the civilized world faced an unparalleled and escalating terrorist threat, and extraordinary measures were required to deal with it. The administration knew all. The people were asked to simply believe what they were told, even though history had taught them that laws were invariably broken when the government indulged in unwarranted secrecy and rejected appropriate constitutional supervision. Where the Bush administration led, other governments followed.[9] From Britain, Italy, and Australia to Russia and China, talk of the terrorist threat became engrained in government polemics. Among the most disturbing examples of this was the Chinese leadership's description of protests by young Buddhist monks in Tibet as terrorist activity.[10]

The Bush inner circle was convinced that operating prison camps outside the United States was useful for a number of reasons. It would be far easier to keep the camps' locations and what went on inside them secret. Since they were not in American territory, the administration argued, they fell outside the jurisdiction of U.S. courts. Congressional approval of how the camps were run, or how detainees were treated there, would not be necessary. Guards deployed could do pretty much what they wanted with their captives. The location of camps built at Guantánamo Bay, land leased from Cuba, was known. However, the conditions inside were not.

For years, news came out drip by drip from individuals who occasionally visited the Guantánamo Bay detention camp. Finally, a Pentagon manual, leaked to Britain's *Guardian* newspaper in November 2007 and published on the Internet, exposed the camp regime.[11] It instructed the guards to keep captives in isolation for two weeks after their arrival to "enhance and exploit the disorientation and disorganization" they felt during the interrogation process. Prisoners were to be "denied basics and access to a Quran," even though almost all of them were devout Muslims, used to daily prayers. And the Pentagon manual made clear that some prisoners were to be denied access to the International Committee of the Red Cross and delivery of ICRC mail, despite statements by the organization to the contrary once such visits began to take place. The ICRC seemed reluctant to disclose it had been denied access, possibility for fear of jeopardizing future visits and risking the perception of its neutrality.

An investigation by the Council of Europe in June 2007 confirmed reports of secret CIA prisons in Europe and other locations, which had first surfaced in 2005. The investigation, conducted by Swiss senator Dick Marty, concluded that "large numbers of people had been abducted across the world" and transferred to countries where "torture is common practice." Others were kept in "arbitrary detention without any precise charge" and without any judicial oversight. Still others had "disappeared for indefinite periods, held in secret prisons, including in member-states of the Council of Europe, the existence and operation of which had been concealed."[12]

Marty reported that these people were subjected to degrading treatment and torture in order to extract information, however unsound, that America claimed "had protected our common security." Prisoners were interrogated ceaselessly and were physically and psychologically abused before being released because they were "plainly not the people being sought." The report said that these were the terrible consequences of the war on terror. It specifically named Romania and Poland as places where the CIA ran secret prisons and torture centers.

How were prisoners taken to such camps, and what was done to them? It turned out that the CIA abducted people, including children as young as seven, across the world. The agency then flew the captives to various secret prisons. The Americans had the right to fly prisoners under an agreement signed by all NATO members, including Britain, that granted blanket overflight clearances to all allied forces involved in the fight against terrorism.[13] In addition to Poland and Romania, prisons were located in other former

Eastern bloc territories, where successors of the dreaded communist intelligence services operated; Chechnya; the former Yugoslav republic of Macedonia; and Syria. Italy was named in the Council of Europe report as a place where the CIA conducted abductions. The report said that the systematic exporting of torture outside the United States and the reservation of such methods exclusively for non-Americans amounted to an apartheid mentality. The exposure of the secret prison system fueled anti-Americanism and created sympathy for Islamic fundamentalism.

Prisoners had been often abducted in foreign countries by local agents for a price. The practice of paying a bounty to kidnappers or informers undermined its credibility, leading to the capture of men younger than sixteen and older than seventy. The prisoners were routinely described by the American administration as "different from us," implying that they did not deserve protection under the law and that their human rights did not matter. Terms such as "aliens," "deadly enemies," and "faceless terrorists" dehumanized them in the eyes of Americans and many worldwide. At a press conference in 2003 President Bush commented, "The only thing I know for certain that these are bad people."[14] The statement was a shattering blow to modern judicial systems, as it failed to acknowledge that a person is innocent until proven guilty and that the burden of proof is entirely on the prosecution. Bush went on to say that he looked forward to working closely with the British government to deal with the issue of these people. Prime Minister Blair, a barrister, stood silently by the U.S. president in the White House.

Does torture work? Sami al-Haj, an Al Jazeera cameraman, was seized on the Pakistani frontier in December 2001, as he and his reporter were on their way to Afghanistan to cover the aftermath of the removal of the Taliban regime. The reporter was lucky, but al-Haj was handed over to the Americans. He was taken to Afghanistan and then to Guantánamo, where he spent the next seven and a half years. In May 2008 he was released with a number of Guantánamo prisoners and flown straight to Khartoum, the Sudanese capital.

Clive Stafford Smith, al-Haj's lawyer and the founder of the international legal action charity Reprieve, describes his client's treatment by his captors in his book on the Guantánamo detainees, *Bad Men: Guantanamo Bay and the Secret Prisons*.[15] Smith writes about beatings in the secret prison at Bagram

Air Base near Kabul; the refusal, despite the doctor's orders, to allow al-Haj to use a support for an injured leg; numerous sessions of interrogation in Guantánamo; the use of sleep deprivation and other harsh techniques; the desecration of the Quran in front of al-Haj; and the interception of communication between al-Haj and his lawyer. This list gives some idea of the kind of regime America set up for foreign prisoners it regarded as "enemy combatants," often without proof. The allegations against al-Haj did not even mention that he worked for Al Jazeera. He had to ask his interrogators what he was supposed to have done wrong. It emerged that his U.S. captors wanted only to turn him into an informant against his employer, which the Bush administration hated for its coverage of news.

Another prisoner, Ibn al-Sheikh al-Libi, alleged to be an al Qaeda leader, was captured in Afghanistan and transferred to the USS *Bataan* somewhere in the Indian Ocean in January 2002. The USS *Bataan* is one of as many as seventeen ships used by the United States as floating prisons, in which detainees were kept and interrogated under torture.[16] About fifty detainees at a time were locked up in the bottom of the isolated ship, and according to one ex-Guantánamo prisoner, they were beaten "even more severely than in Guantánamo."[17] Between torture sessions, they were photographed and seen by a doctor to ensure they would not die and to assess when they could undergo further interrogation. In June 2008, quoting the U.S. government, Stafford Smith said that at least 26,000 people were being held without trial in secret prisons and that as many as 80,000 had been through the secret prison system since 2001.[18] The CIA sent its prisoners to Jordan, Saudi Arabia, Syria, Qatar, and Morocco, as well as Pakistan and Egypt.[19]

Al-Libi spent only a few weeks of his captivity on board the USS *Bataan* before he was sent to Egypt for additional interrogation to extract a confession. Under torture, he gave a statement that Iraq had chemical and biological weapons and provided training to al Qaeda. This was exactly what the Bush administration wanted to hear. In his address to the UN Security Council in February 2003, Secretary of State Powell quoted at length from the "confession" anonymously to make his case for the invasion of Iraq, even though, in a secret report, the CIA had concluded that the information was unreliable.

Al-Libi later retracted the confession, saying it was made under torture, and the American government admitted that the information al-Libi provided was false. At this point a very sick man dying of untreated tuberculosis, al-Libi was sent from Egypt to Libya, where he was said to have committed suicide in his prison. However, Reprieve says there is good reason to believe that al-Libi died of tuberculosis that "developed during his years in U.S. custody."[20] Meanwhile, in Guantánamo, a detainee of little value, an ex–drug addict of Ethiopian origin called Binyam, was being interrogated. He had been sent to Guantánamo from Morocco, where, for eighteen months, he was subjected to torture that his lawyer, Clive Stafford Smith, described as the most horrific he had heard of.[21] His captors in Guantánamo were telling him to give "testimony" against al-Libi and two others—Khalid Sheikh Mohammed and Abu Zubaydah. Binyam had never met any of them.

Powers that operate gulags go to great lengths to keep them under a veil of secrecy. But eventually the secrecy can no longer be maintained. The catalogue of torture techniques used over six weeks on Mohammed al-Qahtani, known as detainee 063, was revealed by *Time* magazine in 2006 and has since been discussed by scholars and legal experts.[22] In June 2004, four months before George W. Bush was to face the American electorate for a second term, his administration struggled in the aftermath of the publication of pictures of naked and hooded prisoners being abused in Iraq's Abu Ghraib prison. The administration was asked to justify "the abandonment of a longstanding prohibition on the use of cruelty by the military."[23] The White House legal counsel, Alberto Gonzales, and the Pentagon's senior lawyer, William J. Haynes, stood before the media to explain that "aggressive interrogation" does work. The case in point was al-Qahtani, who was portrayed as "the worst of the worst."[24] The account of al-Qahtani's treatment tells a story about the Guantánamo regime.

The interrogation log on al-Qahtani contains a record of torture and interrogation sessions longer than twenty hours at a time. For example, one session began in the early hours of the morning. Al-Qahtani was brought into a booth and bolted to the door. A female interrogator began "rapport building," which al-Qahtani found deeply offensive owing to his faith. Exhausted, he eventually fell asleep, only to be woken up by his interrogator. Two hours of further questioning followed, and the detainee asked to pray at dawn. He was refused. He was given water but refused food because he was on a hunger strike. Later in the session, he said he would have a meal. One of his hands was uncuffed to allow him to eat. The female interrogator continued questioning him about the 9/11 attacks. After a two-hour rest, the interrogation resumed. Al-Qahtani complained about his treatment and his mental illness, and said that he missed his brothers. He was told that part of being a man was accepting responsibility for his actions. The underlying message was that he was not a man.

Eight hours had passed since the session began. The prisoner had dozed off. He was woken up and "secured" in his chair. At 11:00 a.m. al-Qahtani asked to pray but the request was again declined. Finally, he was allowed to pray in early afternoon and was offered a meal. He refused to eat. A little after 3:00 p.m., the detainee talked about his family. He asked the interrogator why she was causing him pain by asking him to talk about his family and things he could not have. Two hours later al-Qahtani was offered food and water. He refused the food again. The meal was left next to him.

At 7:00 p.m., seventeen hours after his interrogation began, the detainee was told about the morals of the Quran. He cried and said he wanted to be taken back to Camp Delta, where he would talk. The interrogator, this time a man, told him that he "had to earn his way back to Delta." Just before 8:00 p.m., the interrogator told the detainee that he would help him and not let anything bad happen to him. The detainee was "unresponsive." Half an hour later, the detainee used the restroom and was allowed to sleep. He was awoken an hour later and taken again to the restroom. Then he was "secured" in a chair. He continued to be "unresponsive." At midnight the interrogation was concluded, twenty-one-and-a-half hours after it began.

Al-Qahtani's interrogations continued over forty-nine days—from November 23, 2002, to January 11, 2003. The log published in *Time* magazine described how he was forcibly administered intravenous fluids and drugs and given enemas to keep his body functioning so his interrogation could continue. He was also restrained on a swivel chair, deprived of sleep for long periods, and forced to act like a dog. The temperature in the room was lowered, and cold water was thrown on his face. He was forced to pray to Osama bin Laden. At no point did al-Qahtani confess that he was an al Qaeda member. But his accounts were described as inconsistent, probably because he was tortured for prolonged periods to a degree that could not be measured. On February 11, 2008, al-Qahtani was charged with war crimes and murder by the Office of Military Commissions. He would face the death penalty if convicted. Three months later, the charges against him were dropped. His attorney, Gitanjali Gutierrez of the Center for Constitutional Rights, described the prosecution's use of evidence obtained by torture, hearsay, and secret evidence as "unlawful, unconstitutional and a perversion of justice."[25]

What went on inside the Abu Ghraib prison in Iraq is truly horrific. Up to fifty thousand men, women, and children were kept there at a time. American soldiers poured acid on captives and forced them to remove their clothing, keeping them naked for days in low temperatures and pouring cold water on them. A military policeman had sex with a female detainee. Male prisoners were stripped naked and arranged in a pile so that the American soldiers could jump on them. Soldiers forced male prisoners to wear women's underwear. They took photographs of dead prisoners and threatened captives with rape.[26] Such "blatant, sadistic and wanton" abuses of Iraqis were carried out by American soldiers in the prison, even though, in many cases, the Americans did not know the prisoners' identities or the reasons for their detention.

Other examples of the culture of torture in Abu Ghraib prison are recorded in numerous photographs now in the public domain. A young American soldier, Sabrina Harman, took many of these pictures during her tour of duty inside the prison. Like so many others, she joined the military to help pay for her college education. The *New Yorker* published her story with her photos.[27] The pictures provided a graphic illustration of the mistreatment detailed in the Taguba Report, the official U.S. inquiry into detainee abuse at Abu Ghraib. As a result of the inquiry, a number of low-ranking reservist troops who either took the pictures or were seen in them have since been portrayed as "rogues who acted out of depravity."[28] Documents obtained by the *Washington Post* and the American Civil Liberties Union showed that the senior military officer in Iraq, Lt. Gen. Ricardo Sanchez, authorized the use of military dogs, extreme temperatures, reverse sleep patterns, and sensory deprivation as interrogation techniques in Abu Ghraib.[29]

As the *New Yorker* said, torture at Abu Ghraib "was de facto United States policy," and "the authorization and decriminalization of cruel, inhuman and degrading treatment of captives in wartime have been among the defining legacies" of the Bush administration.[30] The techniques of interrogation were a direct result of the administration's hostility to international law. The doctrine of extracting confessions by torture flowed from the White House, the vice president's office, and a small number of senior Pentagon and Justice Department officials who had essentially become an oligarchy.[31]

REBUKE OF HISTORY

The past is always a rebuke to the present.
—Robert Penn Warren

As fall 2008 approached and George W. Bush's presidency entered its twilight, the administration was fighting on several fronts. In Iraq, the United States had lured Sunni tribesmen away from al Qaeda, which had established itself after the overthrow of Saddam Hussein in 2003.[1] Armed and paid by America, the tribesmen switched their allegiance and were turned into a formidable militia. They came to be described as the "Sons of Iraq" and were organized under the umbrella of the Awakening Council movement. The administration and the media claimed that violence in Iraq had significantly declined, thanks to the U.S. military surge. But the reasons for the decline were far more complex, and among them were the Sons of Iraq. The civil war involving Iraq's various ethnic, sectarian, and political groups had forced many citizens out of mixed communities, leaving enclaves in a fragmented society and less to fight for within them. Meanwhile, America was in the midst of a presidential race dominated by the economic crisis, and the news media had little appetite for Iraq. There was not much interest in keeping a count of Iraqi casualties.

In October the United States transferred the responsibility of paying the salaries of the Sons of Iraq to the Iraqi government and pressed for their integration into the regular army. However, the Shi'a-dominated government in Baghdad—close to Iran—would not agree to integrate more than a fraction of them. It feared a military coup by an Iraqi armed force with a large number of Sunni troops, whose loyalties could not be relied on. A Sunni force could destabilize Iraq, a country with a 60 percent Shi'a population. Having just overcome years of suppression by Saddam Hussein, a Sunni ruler, few Shi'a Iraqis could accept the prospect of a Sunni resurgence to power.

Tensions also grew between the Bush administration and the Iraqi regime over how long the occupation forces would stay in the country and on what terms. Anxiety over reclaiming a legacy for Bush, perhaps the most unpopular president in U.S. history, was evident in Washington. But the creation of a tribal militia by the United States also brought to mind the mujahideen in Afghanistan, who had been armed and financed by the CIA to fight America's proxy war against the Soviet Union in the 1980s and the subsequent civil war among Afghans that led to the emergence of the Taliban.

Throughout 2008 the situation in Afghanistan continued to deteriorate sharply. Attacks by the Taliban and their al Qaeda allies in Afghanistan and Pakistan became more and more audacious. The bombings of the Indian embassy in Kabul in June 2008 and the Marriott Hotel in Islamabad three months later were devastating. Large swaths of Pakistan's frontier provided militant groups with sanctuaries, from which they launched attacks in both countries with increasing frequency. The targets were chosen with precision, and the campaign of violence began to spread to India. A few days before the Islamabad bombing, a series of explosions in the Indian capital, Delhi, killed and maimed scores of shoppers at several locations. There were also attacks in other Indian cities.

These events caused tension between the Bush administration and Pakistan, America's main ally in the region. American pilotless aircraft, flying along the Afghan-Pakistan frontier, were frequently used to attack targets inside Pakistan. They killed not only suspected militants but also civilians. On several occasions, U.S. helicopters carrying troops attempted to land inside Pakistani territory without authorization. Pakistani troops fired on them, and the helicopters had to retreat. The anti-U.S. sentiment had rarely been so strong in the region. The authorities in Pakistan could not afford to allow American troops on their country's soil. The authorities in India, with a Muslim minority nearly as large as the entire population of Pakistan, struggled to decide how far to move toward imposing draconian measures. How did events come to such a pass?

DEBRIS OF THE COLD WAR

For almost half a century after World War II, the United States was at the forefront in efforts to contain communism. By the advent of the 1990s, the Soviet empire was heading toward disintegration. The communist threat was fast disappearing, and America was settling into its new role as the only superpower in the world. Soviet president Mikhail Gorbachev's decision to disengage from client regimes caused a number of governments in the Soviet bloc to fall.[2] Others were left to their own devices.[3] The loss of Soviet influence created new uncertainties in parts of the third world where pro-Moscow rulers had been dominant. The conduct of these rulers in the absence of Soviet restraint was a matter of concern and speculation.

America's proxy war with the Soviet Union in Afghanistan had ended. The strategic importance of the Afghan theater had declined. The Soviet empire's fall meant that the main thrust of American foreign policy in the 1990s was no longer containment of communism. The world had been liberated from the Cold War, and this opened opportunities for America to advance the cause of freedom and capitalism in countries previously under Soviet influence. There was a chance to reshape the world order. But a nuclear power had to be dismantled first.

The USSR was dissolved in December 1991. Within a few weeks, a public demonstration of the new relationship between Washington and Moscow was on display at a Camp David summit attended by the U.S. president, George H. W. Bush, and his Russian counterpart, Boris Yeltsin. The two agreed to a set of principles on which relations between their countries would be founded. They declared that Russia and the United States would no longer regard each other "as potential adversaries." Instead, they would cooperate to prevent the proliferation of weapons of mass destruction and associated technology.

America and Russia admitted that their "conflicts helped divide the world for a generation" but said that they were entering "a new alliance of partners working against the common dangers" they faced.[4] The new relationship was formally described as a "strategic partnership," but the reality was very different. Russia was much smaller and had significantly less power than the Soviet Union. It was in a deep economic and political crisis. The United States realized that, unless Russia was helped to become a modern democratic society, the world would be a more dangerous place.

American worries that the Soviet Union might disintegrate had been growing since the coup attempt against Gorbachev in August 1991.[5] George H. W. Bush was still in the White House and his national security adviser, retired lieutenant general Brent Scowcroft, remained hopeful that the USSR would survive, perhaps as a federation of republics with strong economic and military ties to the center. Otherwise, Scowcroft feared what he described as "atomization," accompanied by "inter-ethnic conflict" with opposing forces pulling the Soviet system in different directions.[6]

These concerns mounted as Russia's authority collapsed and non-Russian republics sought to break away. Reliable estimates indicated that the Soviet Union had about thirty thousand nuclear weapons before it was dissolved.[7] A third of these were long-range strategic nuclear missiles capable of hitting the United States. In addition, there were thousands of tactical weapons such as short-range nuclear missiles, torpedoes, and sea-launched cruise missiles. Following the USSR's demise, Russia, Ukraine, Kazakhstan, and Belarus found themselves with almost all of the long-range strategic weapons.[8] Smaller tactical arms were scattered all over the territory of the Soviet Union, and every republic except Kyrgyzstan inherited them. One nuclear state had suddenly become many. The danger posed by these new states exceeded any situation encountered in the Cold War.[9] America's worst fears were coming true, and something radical had to be done.

The United States needed the Russian leadership to cooperate in the project to neutralize the threat from the Soviet-era weapons and to pull Russia out of the crisis. To make this happen, it was necessary for the West to allow Russia to keep its national pride intact, and the idea of partnership was a way of achieving this.[10] It could be argued that this was among the reasons why America's direct involvement in Afghanistan diminished as the United States increased its involvement in Russia's transformation.

When the Soviet Union was dissolved in December 1991, Gorbachev and Yeltsin assured the U.S. administration that the nuclear weapons would remain under tight central control.[11] Yeltsin was to replace the Soviet leader at the top of the nuclear command, and the other three successor states with Soviet strategic weapons—Ukraine, Kazakhstan, and Belarus—were not to have access to the nuclear codes. Whether this was indeed the case was far from certain. There was particular concern in Moscow over Ukraine's fleet of strategic bombers, which the republic could use to attack Russia with nuclear weapons, if it managed to break the codes on the weapons. A weak and nervous Russia in possession of a vast nuclear arsenal was dangerous. It was also possible that one or more of the other nuclear-armed republics would resort to intimidation and blackmail. Disgruntled, unpaid scientists could sell enriched uranium and plutonium to a rogue state or group.[12] Or the other republics could be lured by foreign countries trying to develop nuclear weapons of their own. Dealing with such risks became a major priority of American foreign policy for the 1990s.[13]

Congress had already laid the foundations for a project to neutralize much of the nuclear arsenal that had once belonged to the Soviet Union in 1991, when it approved a law to prevent the proliferation of weapons of mass destruction.[14] Seven billion dollars were to be spent over the next decade to secure the elimination of such weapons, as well as the materials, expertise, and technologies required to make them.[15] Nuclear warheads were returned to Russia from other former Soviet republics. As a result, Kazakhstan became a nonnuclear state in 1995, and Ukraine and Belarus followed a year later.[16]

All three republics signed the Nuclear Non-Proliferation Treaty, and programs to dismantle long-range missiles and aircraft capable of carrying nuclear weapons continued with American help in Kazakhstan and Ukraine. To avert the possibility of nuclear materials falling into the wrong hands, an agreement was signed in 1993 that allowed the United States to buy uranium from Russia.[17] A plan was made to protect, control, and account for nuclear materials, and a secure storage facility was to be built in Russia under a separate deal.

Two further steps were taken in 1994, a year after Bill Clinton succeeded George H. W. Bush as president. The first Strategic Arms Reduction Treaty (START I) came into force on December 5, 1994.[18] At the same time,

American and Russian laboratories began cooperating with each other to further improve the security of weapons-grade nuclear materials. Under a deal, the United States would help Russia to stop the production of plutonium, and Russian nuclear scientists were to be given assistance to find jobs in the commercial sector. The last nuclear warheads from the other successor states were returned to Russia in 1996.

AMERICA'S OTHER CRISIS: THE IRAQI INVASION OF KUWAIT

The other crisis to dominate American foreign policy in the early 1990s was Iraq's invasion of Kuwait in the oil-rich Gulf.[19] The occupation of Kuwait gave rise in Washington to fears that the Iraqi army could move into Saudi Arabia, a close ally of the West and the most important source of oil for the industrialized world. Articulating such fears, President George H. W. Bush said that what was "at stake was more than one small country." If Saddam's occupation of Kuwait was allowed to succeed, there was a "danger that the world would return to the 1930s," when aggressors ran rampant and the consequence was World War II. America's task therefore was to liberate Kuwait from Iraqi occupation.[20]

To make it happen, America provided military force, and the United Nations provided the legal basis for its use. Other coalition partners, most notably Kuwait and Saudi Arabia, made substantial financial contributions to the war. Japan and Germany, almost totally dependent on imported oil, were at first reluctant to help for fear of risking their supplies from the Middle East. In the end, though, Bush secured "13 billion dollars from Tokyo and 11 billion dollars from Bonn."[21] By early March 1991, the American-led coalition had liberated Kuwait from Iraqi occupation.

CLINTON'S ENLARGEMENT AGENDA

The Democratic ex-governor of Arkansas, Bill Clinton, defeated George H. W. Bush in the November 1992 presidential election and took the oath of office in January 1993. President Clinton's priority was to revive the U.S. economy after years of decline and vast military expenditure. Clinton's national security adviser, Anthony Lake, articulated this idea once Clinton became president. In a speech at Johns Hopkins University on September 21, 1993,

Lake said that, in seeking the presidency, Clinton had promised not only to launch "a domestic renaissance" but also to "engage actively in the world in order to increase our prosperity, update our security arrangements and promote democracy abroad." Lake described the 1990s as an era of "unparalleled opportunity" and championed the "enlargement" of free markets to achieve economic prosperity.[22]

Russia's cooperation was vital for the success of Clinton's plan. Since before his inauguration, Clinton had been receiving intelligence briefings on the mounting parliamentary opposition to President Yeltsin's reform program. The U.S. administration was aware that a conservative takeover in Russia could start a new arms race and sink the entire plan for the American renaissance. Yeltsin "needs friends abroad because he's got so many enemies at home," Clinton said. He told his advisers "to try to keep Yeltsin going,"[23] and the U.S.-Russia collaboration continued throughout the Clinton presidency.

The focus of Clinton's Russia policy was investment, not massive handouts. It continued until an economic crisis forced Yeltsin to default on repayments of foreign debt and to devalue the Russian currency in 1998. As billions of dollars were withdrawn from the Russian economy every month, Clinton pushed the International Monetary Fund to support a recovery program. Within two years, Russia's income from oil sales rose substantially owing to an increase in the world prices, and the crisis subsided.

AFGHANISTAN: THE RISE OF THE TALIBAN

While the Clinton administration was consumed with the crisis created by the Soviet Union's dissolution and the plan for America's economic recovery, conditions in Afghanistan were deteriorating. Toward the end of 1994, a little-known militia called the Taliban came to prominence after capturing Kandahar in southern Afghanistan.[24] Two years after the fall of the Soviet client regime led by Mohammad Najibullah, the Afghan state was rapidly disintegrating. The government of President Burhanuddin Rabbani, which was dominated by the Tajik minority, controlled Kabul, its surrounding areas, and the northeast of the country. Another Tajik commander, Ismail Khan, controlled Herat and neighboring provinces in the west. The Uzbek warlord Abdul Rashid Dostum held sway in northern Afghanistan, while eastern and southern provinces close to Pakistan were under the control of a number of Pashtun commanders. The domain of Gulbuddin Hekmatyar, Pakistan's favorite Afghan warlord, was relatively small.[25]

Afghans had longed for peace for more than a decade, but their hopes had been shattered by the continuing war among the mujahideen. The disappointment was all the greater because many Afghans had expected America to demonstrate the same level of commitment to stabilization and rebuilding that the Reagan administration had shown in confronting the Soviet occupation forces. Instead, there was a rapid decline in America's interest in Afghanistan in the 1990s.

THE ORIGINS OF THE TALIBAN

The Taliban militia rose to power in a vacuum created by the civil war that followed the Soviet client regime's collapse in 1992. Before the communist takeover, Afghanistan had been a nonhierarchical and decentralized society, in large part because about 80 percent of the population belonged to the Hanafi sect, the most liberal of the Sunni schools of thought.[26] Hanafi was based on customary practices and therefore was the easiest version of Sunni Islam to follow. The minority sects were scattered along the fringes of the country, and Afghan communities showed great tolerance toward each other. The war ultimately shattered not only the Afghan state but also the social structure and its inherent tolerance. Other influences grew more dominant in society.

Most of the Taliban were young Afghans who had spent their entire lives as refugees of the war against the Soviet Union. Many were born and grew up in Pakistan. From early on, they had seen adult male members of their families go to fight the communists, holding the Quran in one hand and a gun in the other. Sometimes their fathers, brothers, and uncles returned home after months and went back to fight again, but often they returned ill or seriously injured. Many perished in the conflict. The number of young orphans in Afghan refugee camps rose to hundreds of thousands. Many of these young Afghans had taken part in the final stages of the war against the Soviets. Some in the Taliban leadership had suffered permanent injuries just before the Soviet withdrawal. Their wounds were a constant reminder of the brutality of the conflict around Kandahar, their stronghold, in the late 1980s.[27]

The nearest medical facilities for the injured were a two-day camel ride to Quetta, Pakistan.

Most of the senior Taliban leaders came from poor, disadvantaged backgrounds. The supreme leader, Mullah Omar, was born around 1960 into a landless Pashtun family in Kandahar. Part of his youth was spent in Uruzgan Province, one of the most undeveloped and inaccessible parts of Afghanistan, where Soviet occupation forces rarely went. After the premature death of his father, Omar became responsible for looking after his mother and extended family at a young age. It is known that toward the end of Soviet occupation, Omar was a member of a mujahideen faction, Hizb-i-Islami (Khalis). He was wounded several times between 1989, when the Soviets retreated, and 1992 and lost his right eye in an encounter. It was probably his disability and lack of charisma that made him very shy. Most of his early followers said that they joined Omar not because of his military or political skills but because of his piety and belief in Islam.[28]

As many Taliban members were born and had lived in refugee camps in Pakistan for years, their links with Pakistani society were very close. Their views on a whole range of social and political issues were shaped by the time they spent in Pakistani religious schools, where they had found shelter and studied the Quran and Islamic law. After the mujahideen victory over the communist regime in 1992, some had returned to their homes in southern Afghanistan. Many had stayed back in Pakistan, where they were scattered in Balochistan and North-West Frontier Province. They had their identity cards and continued to receive international refugee assistance. Their children received free education in Islamic schools.

These schools were run by the Jamiatul-Ulama-i Islam (JUI), a fundamentalist party that had built up a strong following in Pakistan's border region by the early 1990s. As the JUI expanded its base, other Islamic groups lost support. The Taliban soldiers were taught a very strict interpretation of Islam, especially in regard to restrictions on women. It forbade any political role for women, but the Taliban took this much further. They outlawed women from education and work. Activists of the JUI were extremely hostile to Shi'a Muslims, whom they regarded as unbelievers. The Taliban were similarly hostile to the Shi'a and other minorities.

The Taliban emerged with promises to end the state of lawlessness and to restore peace and security in Afghanistan. They were eager to expand their control throughout the country and employed extremely coercive measures to suppress all opposition. To legitimize the suppression, they resorted to those parts of the Islamic legal code, Shari'ah, that prescribe severe punishment even for minor offences. Many Afghans were initially attracted by promises to end banditry and extortion by local warlords. Broader manifestations of the Taliban regime, including treatment of women and ethnic minorities, emerged later.

Women were forced to stay indoors, and male doctors were refused permission to treat female patients. Female teachers could no longer teach boys even at elementary schools, and a large number of institutions had to close. The Taliban committed numerous atrocities against Shi'a Afghans, whose loyalty to their country was questioned because of their cultural and spiritual ties with Iran. Relations between the Taliban regime and Iran were severely tested from time to time.

EVOLUTION OF THE TALIBAN-ISI ALLIANCE

Inter-Services Intelligence of Pakistan and the U.S. Central Intelligence Agency had backed hard-line Afghan warlord Gulbuddin Hekmatyar throughout the war against the Soviet Union in Afghanistan. Even after the collapse of the communist regime in Kabul, the ISI continued to support Hekmatyar's push against the Tajik-dominated government in Kabul. By 1994, more than two years of civil war had devastated the Afghan capital, and the prospect of Hekmatyar seizing control of the city was no nearer.

The ISI was also under pressure from the civilian government of Benazir Bhutto. She wanted to open up trade routes to Central Asia via Afghanistan, but this could not be achieved so long as Afghanistan was fragmented. Bhutto had asked her interior minister, Naseerullah Babar, a loyal retired general, to lead an effort to establish whether trade with Central Asia was indeed possible if Afghanistan came under a single authority.[29] Her plan was a direct challenge to the ISI. If Bhutto were to succeed, then the ISI's influence in Afghanistan would greatly diminish.[30] The agency's fears were reinforced when Bhutto met two of Afghanistan's northern warlords, Ismail Khan and General Dostum, in Ashgabat, Turkmenistan, on October 28, 1994, to lobby them for help.[31]

Three weeks before the Taliban captured Kandahar in early November 1994, they fought a battle with Hekmatyar's Hizb-i-Islami at a remote border post, Spin Buldak, an important refueling stop for the transport mafia and a garrison for Hekmatyar's forces. The emergence of petty warlords and Hekmatyar's failure to establish order had generated deep resentment in the local population and traders. The transport mafia had given the Taliban leadership a large amount of money and promised a monthly retainer if the newly emerged militia could clear the roads for traffic and guarantee security. The offer was too good to refuse.

The Taliban launched an attack on Hekmatyar's garrison and defeated his forces after a brief but intense battle. They then seized a large, heavily defended weapons store. There is evidence that Pakistani frontier troops under the direct command of the Interior Ministry helped the Taliban. Declassified American documents show that Pakistani officers on the scene coordinated the operation, and Hekmatyar's base came under artillery fire from Pakistani positions before the Taliban captured the weapons depot.[32] Suddenly, the Taliban possessed large quantities of weapons, ammunition, and military vehicles. The Battle of Spin Buldak changed the course of the Afghan conflict, with consequences few had anticipated at the time. It was the end of the alliance between Pakistan and Hekmatyar.

The Battle of Spin Buldak caused shock waves among militia commanders, but they continued to quarrel among themselves and openly accused Pakistan of supporting the Taliban. Rivalries and confusion grew in Pakistan too, as the ISI and the Interior Ministry competed for influence.[33] Bhutto was determined to take the lead on Afghanistan, but the ISI was not going to be left behind. This explains the composition of a "test convoy" that traveled from Pakistan to the Central Asian Republic of Turkmenistan in October 1994 to demonstrate the viability of a trade route through Afghanistan. It was Bhutto's idea, and Interior Minister Babar planned the journey. More than thirty trucks were driven by ex-Pakistani soldiers specially hired for the purpose. Diplomats from America, Britain, Spain, Italy, China, and South Korea were invited to travel with the convoy to demonstrate to the outside world that the route through Afghanistan was secure and viable. The ISI was not willing to be left behind. A senior officer of the agency, Colonel Imam, was on board, and Taliban commanders with their troops provided security escort.[34]

These developments caused an internal debate in the ISI that lasted for months. While intelligence officers involved in field operations advocated that Pakistan should give more support to the Taliban, those involved in the long-term planning and intelligence gathering wanted to keep the support to a minimum. The ISI high command was short of funds because the usual channels of support from America and Saudi Arabia had dried up and a significant proportion of its resources was being deployed to influence the insurgency in the Indian part of the disputed territory of Kashmir.[35]

The debate came to a conclusion in mid-1995 with a consensus between the ISI and the military to support the Taliban. Pashtun army officers played a key role in achieving the agreement.[36] They were concerned that the Tajik-dominated government in Kabul had become too close to Pakistan's rivals—Russia, Iran, and India. The army had also come to accept that the Taliban were the "only possible alternative" for Pakistan. There was deep distrust between the ISI and the Afghan government's defense chief, Ahmad Shah Masoud, and the agency wanted a strong ally to counter him.[37] The Taliban were seen as the solution.

THE TALIBAN AND SAUDI ARABIA

Taliban successes were not achieved with help from Pakistan alone. Saudi Arabia, too, was drawn in to support the organization. In July 1996 the Saudi intelligence chief, Prince Turki al-Faisal, visited the Pakistani capital, Islamabad, and the Taliban stronghold, Kandahar, to discuss plans to capture Kabul. The prince increased shipments of supplies to the Taliban, and the militia turned its attention not to the capital but to Jalalabad. Saudi Arabia and Pakistan helped engineer the surrender and eventual flight of the head of the ruling council in the city, Haji Abdul Qadir. He was given a large amount of cash and safe passage to Pakistan, with a promise that his assets would not be confiscated.

From then on, the Taliban were unstoppable. By late September their forces had encircled Kabul from three sides, and winter was closing in. The city had endured merciless rocket attacks, punctuated by ground assaults, for months. The defenders were well dug in, but they did not have the numbers to launch counteroffensives and push the Taliban away from the capital. The ISI, meanwhile, kept the Taliban supplied with military hardware and fighters. The agency also played a key role in liaising between the Taliban and Saudi intelligence.

In the end, the pressure from the Taliban, supported by Pakistan and Saudi Arabia, proved too much. On September 26, 1996, President Rabbani's military commander, Ahmad Shah Masoud, ordered his troops to evacuate Kabul. Within hours, columns of Taliban fighters were moving into the Afghan capital. One column went straight into the UN building where Najibullah, the deposed communist leader, had been living since his regime collapsed in 1992. He and his brother were beaten, tortured, and hanged outside the presidential palace.[38] The manner of their execution was shocking and foreshadowed the way the Taliban were going to impose their rule.

THE AFTERMATH

The 9/11 attacks prompted the United States to return to Afghanistan to remove the Taliban regime and destroy al Qaeda, which had been given a safe haven by the Taliban. Overthrowing the Taliban from power was a relatively easy task. Stabilization and reconstruction of the country, neglected for so long after the U.S. proxy war against the Soviet Union, involved many challenges. The Taliban and al Qaeda regrouped and reinforced themselves in Afghanistan and Pakistan. Their top leaders, Mullah Omar and Osama bin Laden, continued to elude capture. Afghans had, at first, welcomed their liberation from the Taliban. But then, many became resentful of the Americans and their use of overwhelming force, which resulted in large civilian casualties and destruction of property.

Indeed the United States was justified in focusing on the threat of nuclear proliferation after the collapse of the Soviet state and using force to liberate Kuwait after its invasion by Iraq. But the neglect of Afghanistan in the 1990s was as much responsible for the rise of groups like the Taliban and al Qaeda as pouring billions of dollars of weaponry into the country in the last phase of the Cold War in the 1980s.

The Bush-Cheney administration, driven by the neoconservative agenda to impose America's will on the Middle East, made a decision to invade Iraq, which had numerous consequences already discussed in this book. One consequence that should, however, be highlighted here is the diversion of vital resources from Afghanistan. The Bush administration essentially opted to ignore Afghanistan after 2003 to focus on Iraq and the oil-rich Middle East. Moreover in prosecuting his war on terror, Bush showed an extraordinary lack of sensitivity for the peoples and cultures of the region. This lack of sensitivity caused America's failure in one of the most volatile parts of the world. And this failure is a reminder that history returns with a rebuke to those who disregard its lessons.

8

DIMENSIONS OF FAILURE

What we need is not the will to believe, but the will to find out.
—Bertrand Russell

As President George W. Bush entered his final year in office and the campaign to elect a successor gathered pace, the record of the Bush administration came under greater scrutiny in 2008. Violence declined somewhat in Iraq
owing to a combination of factors: America's military surge; Awakening militiamen patrolling Sunni areas where they had fought the occupation forces
alongside al Qaeda before; the cessation of hostilities by the militia close to
the Shi'a nationalist cleric, Muqtada al-Sadr; and the influence of Iran, with
which the Iraqi government had developed close ties.

The rise of the Sunni militia began to cause worry among Shi'a communities. Experts maintained that Iraq was still "the most dangerous country
in the world." Playing down killings, America and the Iraqi government had
launched "a largely successful propaganda campaign to convince the world
that things are better in Iraq and that life is returning to normal."[1] However,
there was no such doubt about Afghanistan and its neighbor, Pakistan, where
the campaign of violence by the Taliban and al Qaeda had spread to every
province and spilled over the border into India.

Economic collapse in America and the rest of the world followed in
late 2008. The state of the economy was the primary reason the Republican

Party was defeated in the November election. But before that, crises in Pakistan, Georgia, and elsewhere brought further pressure to bear on George W. Bush, increasing the outgoing president's political isolation. His own party distanced itself from him. He did not attend the Republican National Convention, which nominated Senator John McCain as the presidential candidate and Sarah Palin, governor of Alaska, as his vice presidential running mate. The Republican candidates often criticized the Bush administration during the campaign. Bush had the highest disapproval ratings for any U.S. president and spent most of his time in the White House. This isolation made George W. Bush a lame-duck president but also gave him freedom to pursue his foreign policy agenda away from the limelight of the election campaign.

PAKISTAN

For more than six years after 9/11, President Bush had a close alliance in his war on terror with Gen. Pervez Musharraf. When the tide of opposition to Musharraf became overwhelming, the Pakistani president made efforts to avoid the growing crisis. Elections were held in Pakistan in February 2008 after the country's most charismatic leader, Benazir Bhutto, was assassinated, allegedly by a Taliban suicide bomber. By that time, it was too late for General Musharraf, and he resigned as president in August 2008. Bhutto's People's Party, led by her widower, Asif Ali Zardari, and the Muslim League of former prime minister Nawaz Sharif, who had been exiled by the military regime to Saudi Arabia, emerged as key players in the election.

Showing little regard for Pakistan's internal politics and the sensitivities of its people, the Bush administration backed an alliance between the military and the People's Party to rule Pakistan. After the February 2008 election, a coalition government took office for a few months. It broke down, and Nawaz Sharif pulled his party from the governing coalition in May 2008, leaving America's preferred arrangement in power. Zardari and Sharif had been old political enemies and odd bedfellows, and Zardari knew he, not Sharif, had America's blessings. As soon as Musharraf was forced out of the presidency, the shaky alliance of the two most powerful civilian politicians fell apart. The purpose that brought Zardari and Sharif together in the first place—the removal of Musharraf—had been achieved. Old hostilities came to the fore again.

The sudden outbreak of hope after Zardari's victory in the February 2008 election had not been seen in Pakistan for a long time. The electorate had sent a clear message to those traditionally in control of the country's destiny: to the military, which had ruled Pakistan for more than half of the period since independence in 1947 and which, under General Musharraf, had subverted the judiciary above all, and to America, whose role in shaping Pakistan's policies, through the Bush administration's proxy, Musharraf, was seen as unacceptable interference. After ruling the nation from the front for almost a decade, the military in Pakistan had had enough. It retreated into the background but continued to be the real center of power behind a civilian facade.

As mentioned, Zardari and Sharif were old adversaries. They belonged to very different political clans. Sharif was a protégé of the military dictator General Zia-ul-Haq, who had ruled Pakistan for a decade until he died in 1988. Under his martial law administration, the Sharif family enjoyed a dramatic rise in its business and political fortunes. Zardari belonged to the Bhutto clan by marriage to Benazir. Sharif was from Punjab, the most populous and wealthy province, which dominates the military hierarchy; Zardari was from Sindh, a province with about half the population of Punjab.

In the 1980s Nawaz Sharif's political fortunes rose dramatically, starting with his appointment as chief minister of Punjab, with the blessings of General Zia. Sharif's rise continued after Zia's death, and in 1990 he became the prime minister of Pakistan. Zia, during his military rule, deposed and then executed the head of the Bhutto clan, Zulfiqar Ali, the elected prime minister of the country. Before Sharif and General Musharraf fell out and Sharif's government was deposed in a coup in 1999, it was Sharif who was close to the military establishment. The Bhutto clan was the outcast. Benazir and her husband spent years in jail.

Memories of his overthrow and subsequent exile to Saudi Arabia by Musharraf made Sharif distrustful of the army. Zardari, acknowledging the army's paramount role in Pakistani politics and encouraged by America, wanted to work with both the military and Sharif. In 2008 both Sharif and Zardari were far more mature and not as impetuous as they had been in their youth. But that the political fortunes of one were made at the cost of the other remained a fact of history difficult to forget.

Against that difficult-to-forget episode of history was the reality of 2008. Zardari's People's Party had emerged as the larger party in Parliament, and its character was truly national. The main stronghold of Sharif's Muslim League was Punjab, the most important province but not the whole country. This mattered at a time when rival forces were pulling the country apart, some representing Islamic fundamentalism, others secularism; some supporting a strong center, others demanding greater provincial autonomy. At the end of the Bush presidency, Pakistan was more volatile than it had been in 1971, when East Pakistan seceded to become Bangladesh. Still, the Bush administration had its own agenda for Pakistan.

Zardari and Sharif maneuvered to consolidate their positions after years in the wilderness. Pakistan struggled with the growing insurgency by the Taliban and other armed groups in the country. And the economic crisis worsened, raising new questions. As Zardari embarked on his quest to become the next president of Pakistan, would he turn the post into that of a constitutional figurehead? Or would he insist on keeping the powers to dismiss the government, dissolve Parliament, and meddle with the judiciary?

Would the next president side with the all-powerful military and cooperate with the United States in the war on terror that had caused Musharraf's downfall? Or would he work to reduce the army's role in the running of the country? Would the judges dismissed by Musharraf by illegal means be reinstated? Or would the integrity of the judiciary remain compromised? Above all, would the hopes the people of Pakistan had pinned on their elected politicians be realized? Or would there be disappointment once more?

As it happened, Zardari won the presidency, and the powers accumulated by the military rulers of the past remained with the president. The sacked judges were reinstated in March 2009 when the lawyers' agitation could not be resisted. Foreign aid and remittances from the Pakistani expatriates began to dry up as the worldwide economic crisis deepened. And American air raids on suspected Taliban and al Qaeda hideouts inside Pakistan's lawless tribal belt, unknown in previous years, were launched with increasing frequency. Official protests against violations of Pakistan's sovereignty became weaker. And the impression that the government in Islamabad was helpless to deal effectively with challenges from insurgents and external powers alike grew.

PAKISTAN, INDIA, AND THE BUSH POLICY TURN

While the crisis in Afghanistan and Pakistan worsened, a gradual shift occurred in America's policy in South Asia. Washington came to view India, not Pakistan, as the main bulwark against militancy. After some years of deliberation between the Bush administration and India, the White House pushed for India to be given an unprecedented exemption, so it could join the nuclear club. India had not signed the Nuclear Non-Proliferation Treaty or the Comprehensive Test Ban Treaty and possessed nuclear weapons just as Israel did. After intense lobbying by the Bush administration, the forty-six-member Nuclear Suppliers Group granted a waiver to India. The decision cleared the way for India to buy nuclear components and fuel for use in its civilian power plants.

The International Atomic Energy Agency, the UN watchdog over nuclear activity, and suppliers agreed to do business with India. Thus, the West accepted the reality of the country's nuclear arsenal. The move was an acknowledgment of the strategic environment in which the great powers, America and Russia, and emerging countries and regional players, such as China, India, and Pakistan, had to live. All were rivals as well as allies. The long-term goal of each was to outdo the others economically and militarily. But they had to cooperate in the short run as they pursued their objectives.

America's new approach toward India, a secure democracy, marked the end of Washington's traditional preference for Pakistan, which had been evident during the Cold War and again in the seven years after 9/11. But the rules of the game with India had to be different. The country had a strong democratic system; it was too large and independent to take orders; and it had a strong, rapidly growing economy. Disenchanted with its old ally, Pakistan, America's interests had shifted. India had a capacity to act as a democratic bulwark against terrorism. It provided opportunities for trade. And, in the long run, it would serve as a counter to the growing military and economic power of China.

MIDDLE EAST

George W. Bush paid his last visit to the Middle East as president in May 2008. The trip pleased some in Israel but offended others, including his Arab hosts in Saudi Arabia and Egypt. The reverberations of the visit were felt throughout the region and beyond.

When a head of state visits a region in which enemies live side by side and plans to see them all, it is time to be careful. It is wise not to heap praise on one side if the visiting leader also wants to influence the other side and to play a role in mediation. President Bush's speech to the Israeli parliament in Jerusalem on May 15 was inflammatory. Bush offered no pretense of impartiality when he told the world that "America was Israel's closest ally" and Israel was "a homeland for the chosen people," without acknowledging the plight of the Palestinians.[2]

Barely able to restrain himself, Palestinian Authority president Mahmoud Abbas reminded Bush that 1948, the year Israel was established, was also a year of "catastrophe" for the Palestinian people.[3] The usual Arab courtesy was difficult to maintain. Abbas confronted Bush directly when they met and told him that he, as the U.S. president, had to show balance.

Palestinian newspapers were unanimous in their condemnation of Bush. In two of America's closest allies in the Arab world, Egypt and Jordan, there was severe criticism of the U.S. president. The Egyptian newspaper *Al-Jumhuriyah* accused him of twisting the facts. *Al-Akhbar* remarked that Bush had come to express his bias. This president did not think that his role as the leader of the world's most powerful country "demands neutrality, or at least objectivity." *Al Ghad* of Jordan expressed outrage in an editorial, saying that Bush had come, not to repeat his promise of a Palestinian state, but to celebrate with his Zionist friends the anniversary of a state based on occupation and rape. *Al Arab Al Yawm*, another Jordanian publication, described Bush's speech to the Israeli parliament as full of bigotry. Interestingly, the Syrian publication *Tishreen* was measured in comparison. It ran an editorial that said, "Bush is backtracking on promises he made during the Annapolis conference on the declaration of a Palestinian state" before the end of 2008.

Even Israeli newspapers were uncertain about how to take the U.S. president's explosive intervention. In the view of the *Jerusalem Post*, "Bush didn't have to utter these thoughts. His career is over, he no longer needs Jewish vote." And *Ha'aretz* warned the Israelis, "We should not allow this show of solidarity to go to our heads. Grave dangers lie ahead and no-one can do the job in our stead."[4]

Whether the speech was calculated or simply a misstep was unclear. It certainly was not proper conduct by a visiting head of state. Nor did it help fight the fires in the most politically sensitive region in the world. Bush's assertion near the end of 2008 that "a comprehensive peace settlement in the Middle East is possible" was clearly overly optimistic.[5] And as the president ran out of time, he ran out of friends.

The controversy over his Middle East trip did not end with the speech in Israel. In Egypt, Bush lectured President Hosni Mubarak on democracy and civil liberties, as well as the need to isolate terrorism. He told the Muslim people in the Middle East that Hezbollah, Hamas, and al Qaeda had to be defeated. He warned that the "light of liberty" was at risk from "spoilers such as the regimes in Iran and Syria" and called on the region to reject their policies and prevent Iran from acquiring nuclear weapons.[6] Mubarak, who had been president of Egypt for twenty-five years, did not show up for Bush's speech before the World Economic Forum on the Middle East at the Egyptian resort Sharm el-Sheikh. At the conference Bush told his audience that politics in the Middle East "consisted of one leader in power and the opposition in jail." Bush did not show up to listen to Mubarak when he spoke either.

The message seemed hypocritical given the Bush administration's foreign policy, which used authoritarian regimes mercilessly. So what was behind the president's extraordinary behavior? It was possible that, deep down, George W. Bush realized his own powerlessness to shape events and blamed everybody else for his failures. Or he thought a Democratic victory likely in November 2008 and had no interest in making things easier for the next U.S. president.

America remained absorbed in the presidential campaign and the economic crisis during 2008. Meanwhile, the Israeli-Palestinian dispute escalated. In December, the six-month truce between Israel and the Palestinian group Hamas ended. Hamas, which ruled the Gaza Strip, had won the elections for the Palestinian Legislative Council in 2006. The Israeli blockade of Gaza continued during the cease-fire, and the militant rocket attacks on Israel from the territory declined. On December 27, at the end of the truce, which each side blamed on the other, full-scale hostilities broke out. Israel, asserting its right of self-defense, bombed Gaza for eight days before its forces launched a ground invasion of the territory on January 3, 2009.

Hours before the invasion, and more than two weeks before the end of his presidency, George W. Bush seemed to give the go-ahead to Israel. In a radio address, Bush said that Hamas was a terrorist organization and "no peace deal would be acceptable without tougher action" against it. In the bitter conflict that followed, about thirteen hundred Palestinians, including elderly men, women, and children, were killed before Israel announced a unilateral cessation of attacks three weeks later. More than five thousand had been injured and tens of thousands displaced in an already crowded territory. Gaza's infrastructure suffered widespread destruction. Among the targets of the Israeli offensive were civilian communities, hospitals, and UN buildings. On January 6 the International Red Cross described the situation for the 1.5 million Gaza residents as a "full-blown humanitarian crisis." The UN relief agency echoed this sentiment.

On January 9 the Security Council passed a binding resolution (1860) by a majority of 14-0, calling on both sides to cease fire immediately. The Bush administration, which had helped to formulate the resolution, decided to abstain from the vote at the last minute, and Israel promptly defied the cease-fire call. During a visit to the region in January 2008, President Bush had promised a peace deal by the end of his term. At the end of his presidency a year later, the Middle East was engulfed in a major crisis.

A few days before he left the White House, Bush gave a farewell address to America. The entire speech was a long justification for his wars after 9/11, with no remorse for the extraordinary excesses committed during his eight-year presidency. His departure from office was greeted by widespread protests against Israel and the United States throughout the world.

GEORGIA

The showdown in August 2008 between Russia and the pro-U.S. government of the former Soviet republic of Georgia represented the most serious crisis between Washington and Moscow since the end of the Cold War two decades before. And it pushed the world to the brink of a new cold war. The remote region of South Ossetia in the Caucasus had seceded from Georgia when the Soviet Union broke up in 1991, and a low-level war of attrition had been going on there ever since. A majority of South Ossetian residents had been granted Russian citizenship, and Moscow had considerable influence in the area. South Ossetia was known for its substantial energy reserves, and America's involvement in Georgia had grown under the Bush administration, since a popular revolt, with Western help, in late 2003 ousted Eduard Shevardnadze from power. The Russian leadership saw new Georgian president Mikheil Saakashvili as America's proxy in the region. Saakashvili had studied and worked in the United States in the 1990s.

Amid provocations across enemy lines by both sides, the Georgian military launched a heavy bombardment inside South Ossetia. The regional capital, Tskhinvali, was devastated. Thousands were killed; tens of thousands were injured or became refugees. Russia retaliated by sending a large invasion force, which quickly occupied South Ossetia and parts of Georgia. The conflict caused a sharp deterioration in the American-Russian relationship. The resurgent Russia had put the trauma of the breakup of the Soviet state behind it. The leadership in Moscow was younger, more autocratic, and, owing to its vast energy resources, confident. And it had begun to display a new determination to confront what it considered the Western drive to encircle Russia by enlisting more and more former Soviet bloc countries into the Western military alliance, NATO.

Russia cannot be compared to the Soviet Union of the past. However, it remains a potent U.S. adversary in terms of its nuclear arsenal. In an era of American dominance in the oil-rich Middle East, NATO's continued expansion, from the Baltic states through Hungary, Romania, and the Czech Republic to the Bush administraton's attempts to enlist Georgia and Ukraine, triggered a response from Moscow reminiscent of the last phase of the Cold War. In November 2008, Moscow announced its own measures to counter the U.S. plan to deploy missile defense systems in Poland and the Czech Republic. These would include Russian missiles in the Baltic Sea territory Kaliningrad and electronic equipment to hamper the operation of Western facilities.

The conflict in Georgia was a classic example of proxy war between Russia and America. America had provided weapons, training, and intelligence to the Georgian armed forces. America's involvement, beginning under the umbrella of the war on terror after 9/11, had become much more. If President Bush had his way, Georgia would have been granted membership of NATO as part of the alliance's expansion around Russia. But France and Germany prevailed in their opposition, and the question of Georgia's membership was "postponed." In Western Europe, Georgia was seen as neither a full democracy nor a stable country—the most important criteria for NATO membership. And many had doubts about Saakashvili's ability to make mature decisions.

In an era when America had assumed the right to launch preemptive strikes, it was difficult to see the Kremlin behaving any differently. The prospect of Georgia joining NATO, which might deploy nuclear weapons on Georgian territory, was simply not acceptable to Russia. To understand Moscow's perspective, it is worth remembering the Cuban missile crisis of 1962. During John F. Kennedy's presidency, the deployment of Soviet nuclear missiles in Cuba, just ninety miles from the coast of Florida, brought America and the Soviet Union close to a disastrous war. The Soviet leader, Nikita Khrushchev, was eventually forced to back down. In 2008 Russia was in a similar position to America in 1962. But parallels with Cuba were lost on President Bush.

Saakashvili's decision to order the bombardment of South Ossetia gave the Kremlin a convenient excuse to invade Georgia, just as the Bush administration had found it expedient to invade Iraq in March 2003 based on claims that Baghdad had weapons of mass destruction. Russia had begun to play for bigger stakes in 2008, just as America had in Iraq a few years before. At the height of the conflict, Russian forces occupied about one-fifth of Georgian territory. And Moscow was no longer willing to entertain the idea of Georgia's territorial integrity in any negotiations sponsored by the West.

The U.S.-Russia proxy war in the Caucasus created a serious humanitarian crisis. Georgia's pro-Western leader was humiliated, and the country's chances of joining NATO suffered perhaps a fatal blow. The conflict laid bare the truth that the West could not intervene militarily to protect Georgia from the Russian threat. Article 5 of the North Atlantic Treaty says that an attack on one member-state will be regarded as an attack on the whole alliance, which will use all possible means to protect the member-state under threat. NATO's inability to defend Georgia was a defeat for the West.

President Bush's description of the Russian action as "disproportionate and unacceptable" was not credible in the context of America's own behavior under his administration. Diplomacy was never the Bush administration's strong point. And the strategic blunders in Washington and Tbilisi made the conduct of relations with Russia much more difficult. They created new problems for the next occupant of the White House because they gave rise to the prospect that countries around the world might begin to look to Russia, which was ready to take on the West again.

A BROKEN WEST

For much of the first decade of the new century, the U.S. economy had grown on the back of a housing bubble, just as growth in the 1990s was driven by a boom in the technology sector. House prices rose by as much as 50 percent, after inflation, in the ten years before 2007.[7] The trend was dangerous because there was no equally extraordinary growth in the U.S. population or in personal income. So, how could the housing bubble be explained? Two main factors were responsible: easy loans and cheap goods, manufactured in China and other low-wage economies, which gave Americans a false sense of wealth. As U.S. consumers saw their homes' worth rise dramatically, they borrowed recklessly. Lending was equally reckless, as illustrated by the phenomenon of subprime mortgages. In September 2008 the banking system collapsed, and a deep economic crisis followed. America's recession quickly became a worldwide crisis, and the international stock markets crashed.

October 7 was a day of panic on both sides of the Atlantic. The New York Stock Exchange suffered further massive losses, despite a $700 billion government rescue package. In London, shares in the banking sector collapsed, some falling by as much as 40 percent. The chairman of the U.S. Federal Reserve, Ben Bernanke, warned of an impending meltdown. And George W. Bush, whose presidency looked destined for an ignominious end, pleaded for coordinated action by the leading industrialized countries. The International

Monetary Fund estimated financial losses of around $1.5 trillion. They could be higher.

Several major countries' central banks announced cuts in their interest rates after weeks of indecision, during which each country seemed to be engaged in domestic firefighting. America's rescue package was for its institutions, although, if successful, it would benefit others. On October 8 the British government announced a bailout plan of its own. It would spend up to £50 billion in return for "preference shares" in eight of the largest British banks and would guarantee all personal loans. The measure gave the government some control over the banking system. There would also be restrictions on huge executive salaries and generous dividends to shareholders, which had caused strong public resentment.

In the immediate run, individual governments did what was best for their own economies rather than for the global system. In Europe, the Irish Republic, Greece, Spain, Germany, and Britain all took unilateral action. A proposal from French president Nicolas Sarkozy for a common European fund for economic bailout did not find support. The economic crisis shattered what was left of the idea of unity in the European Union, especially among members in the euro currency zone. In the longer run, the era of loose regulation seemed to be over, despite repeated insistence by the outgoing Bush administration to the contrary.

The unfolding crisis completed a catastrophic loss of trust in the West that went beyond economics and finance. If those in power in Washington, London, and elsewhere could not be trusted on the critical matters of war and peace, law and justice, and the treatment of different sections of their own populations, their ability in other areas was bound to be questioned. The leaders of America and its allies had become consumed by a doctrine that left their economies at home to be run by large private institutions that they had befriended, while their attention was focused on wars being fought abroad.

America financed its foreign wars with money borrowed from China and the oil-rich Gulf states. Instead of easy access to the oil fields of the Gulf, the U.S.-led expedition achieved turmoil in the region and beyond. The turmoil contributed to dramatic rises in oil prices that strained the world economy.

And countries like China, Russia, and Saudi Arabia, which had accumulated huge reserves of U.S. dollars, stopped trusting the West. The Arab world resented the West for its treatment of Muslims. The government of Iceland bitterly criticized its "friends" for not doing enough to help after the collapse of the Icelandic financial system and began to look toward Russia for support. The West was broken—economically, politically, morally.

9

POWER WITHOUT PRUDENCE

> You must not lose faith in humanity. Humanity is an ocean; if a few
> drops of the ocean are dirty, the ocean does not become dirty.
> —Mahatma Gandhi

Mahatma Gandhi, the father of modern India, deliberately chose a basic life-style to be close to the masses. Colonialism, poverty, racism, xenophobia—nearly every social ill he saw worried him. Gandhi's propensity to agonize and feel pain wherever he saw violence, suffering, injustice, and double standards made him appear a deeply pessimistic leader. But beneath his pessimism, a fountain of hope lay eager to explode. If Gandhi were alive today, he would feel sorrow over the events since the 9/11 attacks, and he would have constantly agonized over their impact on humankind.

FALLING OUT OF LOVE

The world fell out of love with America during the war on terror declared by President George W. Bush. Much of the sympathy and popular support witnessed immediately after 9/11 faded away, overtaken by news about the Guantánamo Bay detention camp, Abu Ghraib prison, and officially sanctioned torture. It is surprising how quickly goodwill capital and a strong economy can be squandered. The events of 9/11 plunged the world into a climate of fear and insecurity. Yet respect for the rule of law, the principle that an individual is innocent until proven guilty, and, above all, proportionality in the use of force remain core beliefs for many people. America continues to be admired all over the world as a land of freedom and opportunity, a laboratory for scientific and technological advances, and a country capable of doing good. But its policies under the Bush administration generated strong opposition and apathy and created waves of anti-Americanism. Large parts of humanity began to question America's capacity to help countries in need.

The neoconservatives who came into the administration with President Bush in January 2001 were staunch believers in America's military power and in using it to impose their will elsewhere in the world. America is a hyperpower, but the Bush administration's determination to rely primarily on America's military strength to impose its foreign policy led to devastating consequences. The order should have been reversed: soft power should be backed by hard power only when necessary.

The years of the Bush presidency will be remembered as a period of history stained by contradictions between America's values and its actions. The war on terror demonstrated that even a hyperpower can overreach itself, lose control, and hemorrhage political credibility and economic assets. Historically, America has stood for democracy, individual freedom, human rights, open market, and free trade. Inconsistencies can be identified in all administrations. But problems created by the Bush administration were acute and self-inflicted. George W. Bush was inclined only one way—toward using military power to force others to conform.

The neoconservatives' agenda was to impose democracy, but only on those countries that they did not like. The list included Afghanistan, Iraq, and, if events had gone their way, Iran and Syria. The ambition to bring democracy, however, did not apply to Saudi Arabia—which has one of the most oppressive regimes in the world and the biggest base of support for al Qaeda. Since the Saudi royal family has been a U.S. ally and happily sells oil to America, Saudi Arabia did not appear on the "democracy agenda." In Pakistan, democracy was a good idea, but not when parties opposed to the ruling military junta won the elections in 2008. President Bush viewed Pakistan's fledgling civilian government with suspicion. His inclination to do business with the all-powerful military remained strong. When opposition to the military regime became unstoppable, Bush preferred one side, the Bhutto-Zardari clan, over others.

The Bush administration kidnapped numerous "suspects," many of whom were innocent, across the world. The CIA flew them to detention centers like the one in Guantánamo Bay and to other countries, where they were tortured until they made confessions, many of them false and inadmissible in courts. The administration did not acknowledge that Saudi Arabia was a major hideout for active and potential al Qaeda members. Yet Iran, along with Iraq and North Korea, was reviled as part of the "axis of evil" for sponsoring terrorism and running a secret nuclear program. And, astonishingly, North Korea was removed from the U.S. State Department's list of countries supporting terrorism in the final months of the Bush presidency. The desire to claim a successful legacy prevailed over reality. Bush tolerated lack of democratic rule, human rights abuses, and growing militancy in countries that were prepared to collaborate to reach mutual aims. He saved denunciations and aggression for others. When the burden of double standards becomes too heavy, erosion of moral and real authority follows.

America needed more than two decades to come to terms with the legacy of its defeat in Vietnam. The process was helped by two factors: the end of the Cold War and the interlude provided by a comparatively antiwar president, Bill Clinton. The election of George W. Bush in November 2000 was a retreat into history. It took America back to the 1990s, when, some felt, it had failed to make that last push into Iraq to overthrow Saddam Hussein in the Gulf War of 1991. President Bush wanted to punish Iran, but the chaos in Iraq after the 2003 U.S. invasion enhanced Iran's status in the Gulf region. Iran is a difficult country to deal with, but America's difficulties were compounded by the Bush administration's uncompromising, aggressive, and unhelpful attitude. It should have worked with the International Atomic Energy Agency and its director general, Mohamed ElBaradei, instead of undermining its authority by spreading rumors that the United States or Israel would take unilateral action against Iran's nuclear program.

The world embarked on a destructive path on September 11, 2001. Eight years on, the consequences of abandoning the norms of international behavior were evident. The general consensus in the wake of the 9/11 atrocities held briefly. Then, it fell apart as the United States decided to embark on a unilateral course to invade Iraq, against the advice of the chief UN weapons inspector, Hans Blix, and without the Security Council's specific approval. The invasion of Iraq was a devastating blow to UN authority. America's political Right, which had been attacking the world body for years, finally succeeded in reducing its role to that of a mere observer. But when the occupation forces began to encounter resistance and the situation deteriorated, the Bush administration was forced to seek cover of UN approval to remain in Iraq.

Actions of such enormity cannot pass without consequences. By 2008 Russia and China were no longer prepared to let America brandish its power unchallenged. Both permanent members of the Security Council used their veto to kill a draft resolution to impose an arms embargo on Zimbabwe and financial and travel restrictions on President Robert Mugabe and senior members of his regime, for carrying out a campaign of violence to eliminate the opposition.[1] It was a message to America that it could not take for granted the wider international community's support for U.S. actions in other parts of the world.

Is this the beginning of a new era of collaboration between Moscow and Beijing against the United States? Russia has emerged from the shock of losing its superpower status. Its mood is assertive, encouraged by its vast energy resources and the West's vulnerability. China continues to build its power beyond its immediate neighborhood, in Asia and Africa. And India has begun to catch up. The war on terror has made America indebted to China like never before. The Bush administration's decision to fight the war entirely on credit means that future generations will have to bear its costs.[2]

Was the war aimed at completing unfinished business in Iraq after the 1991 Gulf War and getting rid of Saddam Hussein? If so, it amounted to an American president's ego trip. Or was it about security? In that case, it has been a misconceived and mismanaged adventure. It divided the world, damaged the UN system, and made a mockery of long-established conventions on human rights, fairness, and justice. One hopes that such regression can be reversed. And if the war was about oil, a fast diminishing commodity, then it was an unforgivable act of misjudgment with enormous costs.

AN AMERICAN REVOLUTION

The victory of Barack Obama in the 2008 presidential election was akin to a revolution in America. It was a revolution not only because of its symbolism, undeniable though it is. The entry of a black man into the White House 143 years after slavery was abolished by the Thirteenth Amendment to the U.S. Constitution is a powerful symbol. Progress of this magnitude is the result of a monumental struggle, often by people whose names will not receive the recognition they deserve.

A revolution, however, must go beyond such boundaries. It must be a wider response to critical problems in society, an acknowledgment by the masses that things have got to change or there will be a greater calamity. A revolution is not a coup d'état, a seizure of power by a small group of people. It is a wider phenomenon that happens when the time is right. The 2008 election in America reflected all of this and much more. The eight years of Bush's presidency illustrate what damage can be done when the world's most powerful nation goes rogue, squandering its capacity to do good.

I belong to a generation born just after World War II. As someone who has lived and worked in America, traveled from coast to coast, and kept a keen eye on its politics, I have an abiding interest in the country. With sadness, I say that I cannot recall a more repressive period in America's domestic and foreign affairs than the presidency of George W. Bush. The facts speak for themselves.

At home, a mismanaged economy, driven down by hugely expensive foreign wars, crushed middle-class America. A growing number of Americans struggled to stay above the poverty line. In real terms, their plight invited comparisons with the underdeveloped countries of the third world, as they lacked food, nourishment, health care, education, job opportunities, and security. The United States alienated itself from the world through its use of devastating military power and discredited client regimes. The scale of this repression affected the lives of hundreds of millions of people. Such behavior sacrificed friends and inflamed armed opposition, leading to stronger retaliation. The importance of prudence in the employment of power had never been greater than it was at the end of George W. Bush's presidency.

The war on terror has often made me reflect on something said by Mahatma Gandhi, who inspired leaders like Martin Luther King Jr. and Nelson

Mandela: "What difference does it make to the dead, the orphans and the homeless whether the mad destruction is wrought under the name of totalitarianism or the holy name of liberty and democracy?" Those who associate revolutions with the old-fashioned armed struggle in Russia or China in the first half of the twentieth century miss the point.

A revolution is not necessarily a violent event. It is a definite and an overwhelming response against the existing order by people who feel they have had enough. This is what happened in America in 1776, what Americans celebrate on the Fourth of July every year, when the colonies declared independence from Britain. The abolition of slavery in 1865 was also a revolutionary event. So was the introduction of civil rights laws in the 1960s. In Europe, a number of Soviet bloc countries underwent peaceful "velvet revolutions" in the 1980s and 1990s.

The scenes across America on November 4, 2008, were part of a phenomenon of profound magnitude. The voter turnout—over 120 million people—was unprecedented and will be remembered for a long time. The margin of popular votes for Barack Obama was 52–46 percent—less than some opinion surveys had predicted, but still substantial. Obama's majority in the Electoral College, which actually elects the president, was more than 2-1. And the Democrats strengthened their hold by sizeable margins in both chambers of Congress. The verdict was overwhelming.

Writing in *Time* magazine, Nancy Gibbs argued that Obama's victory was not achieved because of the color of his skin, nor in spite of it. "He won because at a very dangerous moment in the life of a still young country," she said, "more people than have ever spoken before came together to try to save it." Gibbs's comments were all-encompassing. They told the story of a superpower falling on hard times, nearly two decades after it had defeated the Soviet Union in the Cold War and thought the capitalist system had won for good.

Although the scale of the Democratic victory in the 2008 election was truly unprecedented, it would be prudent to introduce a note of caution. I know of no revolution fulfilling all that it promised. Obama has been left the arduous task of fixing America's broken system. George W. Bush left the country with a total debt of $10 trillion and a budget deficit of more than $750 billion. In a deepening recession, hundreds of thousands of Americans were losing their jobs every month, while Europe and the rest of the world were also suffering. The Bush administration had chosen to fight three wars—in Afghanistan, in Iraq, and a global war on terror. Dealing with these wars in the short run with a view to ending them eventually—hopefully before too long—was going to be a mammoth job. Fractured relationships abroad needed to be rebuilt, and engagement with international organizations needed to be revived. The most profound lesson of unilateralism: the loss of international support for America weakens its leadership and makes it less effective in the world.

Obama's most urgent task was economic revival, beginning with the restoration of the financial system. But in the longer term, America needed an enlightened approach to medical care, security, and social welfare. The number of people incarcerated in American prisons was 2.3 million. At least 5 million more—the vast majority of them from black and other ethnic minority groups—were on probation or parole. China, with four times the population of the United States, had fewer inmates in jail—around 1.5 million.[3]

What is the total cost of all this, and can anything be done? Consider the failure of the justice system, which relies heavily on plea bargaining to secure convictions. The system convicts some of the most disadvantaged citizens, who have little or no chance of proper legal representation. Innocent people are convicted, incarcerated, and executed. There is miscarriage of justice. Consider, too, the lax gun laws and the violent incidents that lead to avoidable deaths and injuries and massive hospital bills. Two-thirds of Americans have insufficient medical coverage or none at all for at least part of each year.[4] And these numbers are rising as more people become jobless. How many of the sick and the incarcerated die prematurely or spend long years in prison, failing to contribute their best to America? These issues must be taken seriously in Washington. If America doesn't address them, it will become a failing state.

A WEB OF CRISES

The three-day carnage in Mumbai inflicted by young, well-trained gunmen beginning on November 26, 2008, was another gruesome chapter in the most complex web of problems to bedevil the world since the end of the Cold War. As the bloodbath in India's main commercial center was played out on television screens across the world, people who had followed events in New York and Washington, London and Madrid, Islamabad and Bali immediately connected with the escalating terrorism. India is no stranger to terrorism. Still, the killing and wounding of hundreds of people of many nationalities went beyond most Indians' worst fears.

The Indian economy, already caught in the global recession, felt the impact of the carnage. Tourism and investor confidence suffered, at least in the short term. The political fallout went beyond the resignation of the home minister, Shivraj Patil. As a national election approached, the governing coalition led by the Congress Party came under heavy criticism from Hindu nationalists, as well as other sections of Indian society.

There had been a backlash against Muslims in the United States and Europe after 9/11. Violence against India's Muslim and Christian minorities had been on the increase before the Mumbai carnage. And the authorities had faced criticisms for their failure to protect the citizens. Despite fears of a backlash, the Mumbai massacre produced a general sense of revulsion across the country. As seen on television debates, the views were polarized, but there was no appetite for revenge. India is home to 150 million or so Muslims, and though it is a secular country, harmony among its diverse communities has not always been guaranteed. Muslim opposition to Indian rule in Kashmir, which is divided between India and Pakistan, has been a serious problem for the central government. Harsh measures to suppress the militancy fuel popular discontent even more.

As investigations into the massacre began, there were accusations and counteraccusations within the governing coalition and between the opposition and the government. Relations between India and Pakistan plunged following reports that the gunmen may have come by sea from Pakistan and belonged to a militant group, Lashkar-e-Taiba, based there.[5] The attackers had AK-47 assault rifles, manufactured in abundance on Pakistan's western frontier, where groups like the Taliban and al Qaeda have sanctuaries and training camps. The gunmen's sustained ruthlessness and cold-blooded determination to kill until the end was a product of a hardened, well-trained frame of mind.

The president-elect of the United States, Barack Obama, had made the economy his number-one priority upon taking office on January 20, 2009. The massacre in India made his task more complex, even before his inauguration.

Claims of improvement in Iraq were no longer enough to reduce America's engagement in the Middle East so that it could concentrate on the Afghan theater and rebuilding the U.S. economy.

The truth is that the web of crises spans from Palestine through Iraq, Afghanistan, and Pakistan to India and further east. The combination of extreme remedies applied as part of the war on terror and neglect of the real issue in the Middle East—the Palestinian crisis—by the Bush administration has added fuel to the fire. The mistakes have alienated many decent, ordinary people. The same old condemnations of "uncivilized terrorists" and perfunctory support for their victims seem increasingly meaningless. A strong sense of alienation, humiliation, and injustice pervades the Middle East and South Asia. When the situation is so volatile, local crises feed each other until they become a catastrophe. The chain of events in recent years illustrates the way in which many problems become one.

As the day of transfer of power from Bush to Obama approached, 1.5 million Palestinians remained cut off in the Gaza Strip, virtually imprisoned without sufficient food, fuel, and medicine. More than a million of them are registered as refugees with the United Nations. The Israeli blockade of Gaza may have been aimed at breaking the will of its people to support Hamas, which won the parliamentary elections for the Palestinian Authority in 2006. But it had the opposite effect. Desperate people resort to desperate measures. Underground tunnels were soon built to connect Gaza to Egypt to secure access to essential goods and weapons. The humanitarian situation demanded urgent and extraordinary measures to prevent the residents of the territory from reaching the point where their desperation was beyond containment.

The Palestinian problem is central to the wider crisis in West and South Asia. Its solution requires historic efforts involving America and Russia, as well as regional powers including Syria, Iran, Turkey, Egypt, Saudi Arabia, Pakistan, India, and China. Obama has repeatedly offered friendship and support to Israel—a political necessity for any successful American politician. The time has come to exercise a restraining influence on the Israelis. During the campaign, Obama said that he was willing to negotiate with Iran, which has a nuclear program. In Afghanistan and Pakistan, the United States has confirmed indirect talks with the Taliban through Saudi Arabia.[6] Israel has done the same with Syria. In the light of these overtures, the refusal to hold talks with Hamas does not make sense.

The rest comes after the Palestinian problem. Following prolonged negotiations, the timetable for America's military withdrawal from Iraq is set. It is to be completed by the end of 2011, provided unforeseen events do not frustrate the plan. Iran's cooperation is essential to success in stabilizing both Iraq and Afghanistan. But the more hawkish the U.S. administration becomes, the less chance there is of securing that vital support. At the same time, the cooperation of Syria, another big player in the Middle East, is essential for progress in Lebanon and elsewhere.

The crisis across the triangle that includes Afghanistan, Pakistan, and India has both distinct and common aspects. The Taliban represent an indigenous tribal movement in the Afghanistan-Pakistan frontier and will be difficult to eliminate. But it is possible to influence Taliban leaders if conditions are right in both countries and Washington shows willingness to listen to regional experts. America has been heavily involved in both Afghanistan and Pakistan for almost three decades. It played a role in the war. Now it needs to play a part in reconstruction and stabilization. Last but not least is Kashmir, a territory India and Pakistan have disputed since their independence from Britain in 1947. The prospects of a resolution to this intractable problem could improve with democratic reforms in Pakistan and with America's engagement with Pakistan's civilian political establishment. Reforms are also needed on the Indian side of Kashmir, where a combination of political failures and heavy-handed military tactics over many years has fuelled popular disaffection and strengthened the militants.

All this was far too complicated for George W. Bush. Manipulating the public with fear tactics to hasten its approval of punishment for those the White House did not like was the trademark of his administration. Bush's green light to Israel to invade Gaza was part of his broader war in the Middle East—war not only against Hamas and Gaza and Hezbollah and Lebanon, but also against Iran and Syria. In view of the close security ties both Tehran and Damascus have with Russia and China, the potential risks of escalation were even greater. However, all that was not obvious to the Bush White House. An instinctive demolisher, Bush inspected the vast wreckage around him at the end of his presidency and decided to go out with a bang.

Epilogue

[The Bush administration] has left us a legacy that is unsustainable.
—President Barack Obama

Moments after taking the oath of office, President Obama articulated in his inaugural address the legacy he had inherited and the enormity of the task ahead. The nation was at war, and its economy had been badly weakened by greed and irresponsibility. Obama acknowledged that "power alone cannot protect us, nor does it entitle us to do as we please." Power grows through "prudent use of force" and "the justness of our cause." And in a severe rebuke to his predecessor, who sat a short distance away, the new president said that the time had come to set aside childish things. "Greatness is never a given," said Obama. "It must be earned."[1]

No symbol of the arbitrary nature of the Bush-Cheney administration, its abuse of power, and its regime of torture was more powerful than the Guantánamo Bay detention camp. Two days after his inauguration, President Obama issued a landmark executive order, "Ensuring Lawful Interrogations." It revoked all directives, orders, and regulations inconsistent with the new order since September 11, 2001. Obama's new executive order was "to improve human intelligence-gathering, to promote the safe, lawful and humane treatment of individuals in United States custody, to ensure compliance with the treaty obligations of the United States, including the Geneva Conventions, and to take care that the laws of the United States are faithfully executed."[2] He followed up with an order to close Guantánamo and all overseas detention centers run by the CIA.

Obama was an opponent of the Iraq War before it was launched. On October 2, 2002, as the Bush administration prepared for the invasion, the young Illinois senator described it as a "dumb war" in a speech at the Federal Plaza in Chicago. Saddam Hussein was a "brutal man" but posed "no imminent and direct threat to the United States." "In concert with the international community," Obama said, "he can be contained until, in the way of all petty dictators, he falls away into the dustbin of history."[3] Events were to prove opponents of the Iraq War right. On becoming president, however, Obama was no longer a mere objector. The responsibility of extricating America from the costly wars in Iraq and Afghanistan fell onto his shoulders.

As George W. Bush prepared to leave the White House, he signed a U.S.-Iraqi security agreement in November 2008 that envisaged a complete American troop withdrawal by the end of 2011, citing improvements in the security situation. But long-term concerns for the Iraqi state lingered. On March 9, 2009, as the United States and Iraq announced that the withdrawal would be accelerated, a suicide bomber blew himself up in Baghdad, killing about thirty people and wounding many more. Violence had become part of day-to-day life in Iraq.

For President Obama and the United States in 2009, the main foreign policy task was to pacify the complex web of crises in the Middle East and South Asia. The Bush-Cheney administration's war on terror has turned the region into a disaster area that extends from the Israeli-Palestinian conflict to Iraq and Afghanistan to Pakistan, with ramifications for India and further east. Revival of America's economy and faith in its leadership depend on success in reconciliation with adversaries across a volatile landscape.

Where must Obama begin? The conflict between Israel and the Palestinians is an old, festering wound. Neglect of the Palestinians and total support for Israeli actions by the Bush-Cheney administration opened up that wound even more. Israel's war on Gaza was a particularly low point. Moving from that extreme position toward the center is of utmost importance for America. This requires a genuine recognition of the Palestinians' suffering and their legitimate rights as a free people. The Palestinian militants have to do the same for Israel.

The conciliatory tone in America's language after Obama's ascent to the presidency was remarkable. There were encouraging developments: the appointment of George Mitchell as Obama's special envoy to the Middle East; America's billion dollar aid for the reconstruction of Gaza after the war; the new president's desire to improve relations with Iran and Syria; and the general tone in support of fair play. The Hamas leader, Khaled Meshal, hailed the reversal as a "new language," saying that an official opening to his organization was only a matter of time. The wound would take a long time and laborious efforts to heal, but there was hope once again.

"New language" alone cannot provide solutions. The United States needs to restrain Israel, its close friend and ally. As the end of 2009 approached, this was looking increasingly difficult. The right-wing Israeli government of Prime Minister Benjamin Netanyahu continued to resist Obama's demands to halt the expansion of Jewish settlements in the occupied West Bank and East Jerusalem. Previous concessions on the part of Israel have been inadequate, often illusive. There must be enough for the Palestinians to make their homeland a viable state. Otherwise, there cannot be peace and security for either side. Progress toward a resolution of the Palestinian issue would go a long way toward eliminating the main grievance in the Muslim world. It would make a difference in other trouble spots.

With Iran, Obama's offer of a "new beginning" marked a sea change in American policy since the Islamic revolution in 1979. Memories of the overthrow of the pro-U.S. shah of Iran haunt America. In Obama's Iranian New Year message to the Iranians, he called them a "great people" who have a "great civilization."[4] He offered a fresh start and acknowledged that Iran was much more than its recent turbulent history and its animosity toward Washington. Still, many hurdles remained. Accusations of fraud in Iran's June 2009 presidential election, which the incumbent Mahmoud Ahmadinejad won by a large majority, triggered protests. The Iranian government's clampdown against the opposition brought demands in the United States for a harder line to be taken against Tehran. And the question of Iran's nuclear program continues to be a major hurdle to good relations between the two countries.

America renewed its sanctions against Iran following Obama's inauguration—an annual event in the U.S. foreign policy calendar. But sanctions cannot continue if relations are to improve. An eventual deal between Washington and Tehran, whereby America lifts the sanctions in return for Iran's agreement to open its nuclear program to international supervision, would be a major breakthrough. Iran and Syria are significant regional powers. The cooperation of both is vital for the stabilization of Iraq. Iran also could help calm tensions in Afghanistan, Lebanon, and elsewhere.

The need for America to redefine its objectives in Afghanistan and Pakistan is long overdue. As Defense Secretary Robert Gates transferred from one administration to another, he said that America's goals should be more limited.[5] Richard Holbrooke, Obama's special representative to Afghanistan and Pakistan, suggested that too many broad and wild claims had been made in the past. Holbrooke said, "The victory, as defined in purely military terms, is not achievable, and I cannot stress that too highly. What we are looking for is the definition of our vital national security interests." He advocated diplomacy putting "Afghanistan and Pakistan into a larger regional context ... to stabilize this volatile region."[6]

President Obama addressed U.S. foreign policy in the post-Bush era on the CBS program *60 Minutes* in March 2009. His mission in Afghanistan would be "making sure that al Qaeda cannot attack the US homeland and US interests and our allies."[7] It was a dramatic departure from George W. Bush's policy. Displaying raw intensity, Bush had asserted after 9/11 that "there were no rules." His message to the Taliban: "We are going to smoke them out."[8] Obama's preferred objective in Afghanistan and Pakistan was to separate the Taliban from al Qaeda, the former an indigenous phenomenon, the latter an external one. It would make it easier to engage with the Taliban opposition. The idea of the Taliban functioning as a political party, able to play a role under the constitution, no longer seemed impossible. But it turned out to be much more difficult in practice. America's military engagement in Afghanistan and Pakistan intensified within months of President Obama taking office, and 2009 turned out to be the bloodiest year since the American invasion in 2001. Problems also mounted on the political front. The credibility of the presidential election, in which Hamid Karzai was seeking another term, lay in tatters after widespread ballot rigging, Taliban threats, and indifference among Afghan voters.

American exceptionalism and unilateralism are things of the past. The age of regional diplomacy has arrived. For diplomacy to happen, the United States must work to repair its ties with adversaries. It should take greater account of its allies and seek new ones. All this is vital if there is to be no "perpetual drift," and if there is to be the "exit strategy" from war that Obama's America, in deep economic crisis, longs for.

Appendix A:

Project for the New American Century Statement of Principles

JUNE 3, 1997

American foreign and defense policy is adrift. Conservatives have criticized the incoherent policies of the Clinton Administration. They have also resisted isolationist impulses from within their own ranks. But conservatives have not confidently advanced a strategic vision of America's role in the world. They have not set forth guiding principles for American foreign policy. They have allowed differences over tactics to obscure potential agreement on strategic objectives. And they have not fought for a defense budget that would maintain American security and advance American interests in the new century.

We aim to change this. We aim to make the case and rally support for American global leadership.

As the twentieth century draws to a close, the United States stands as the world's preeminent power. Having led the West to victory in the Cold War, America faces an opportunity and a challenge: Does the United States have the vision to build upon the achievements of past decades? Does the United States have the resolve to shape a new century favorable to American principles and interests?

We are in danger of squandering the opportunity and failing the challenge. We are living off the capital—both the military investments and the foreign policy achievements—built up by past administrations. Cuts in foreign affairs and defense spending, inattention to the tools of statecraft, and inconstant leadership are making it increasingly difficult to sustain American influence around the world. And the promise of short-term commercial benefits threatens to override strategic considerations. As a consequence, we are jeopardizing the nation's ability to meet present threats and to deal with potentially greater challenges that lie ahead.

We seem to have forgotten the essential elements of the Reagan Administration's success: a military that is strong and ready to meet both present and future challenges; a foreign policy that boldly and purposefully promotes American principles abroad; and national leadership that accepts the United States' global responsibilities.

Of course, the United States must be prudent in how it exercises its power. But we cannot safely avoid the responsibilities of global leadership or the costs that are associated with its exercise. America has a vital role in maintaining peace and security in Europe, Asia, and the Middle East. If we shirk our responsibilities, we invite challenges to our fundamental interests. The history of the twentieth century should have taught us that it is important to shape circumstances before crises emerge, and to meet threats before they become dire. The history of this century should have taught us to embrace the cause of American leadership.

Our aim is to remind Americans of these lessons and to draw their consequences for today. Here are four consequences:

- we need to increase defense spending significantly if we are to carry out our global responsibilities today and modernize our armed forces for the future;
- we need to strengthen our ties to democratic allies and to challenge regimes hostile to our interests and values;
- we need to promote the cause of political and economic freedom abroad;
- we need to accept responsibility for America's unique role in preserving and extending an international order friendly to our security, our prosperity, and our principles.

Such a Reaganite policy of military strength and moral clarity may not be fashionable today. But it is necessary if the United States is to build on the successes of this past century and to ensure our security and our greatness in the next.

Elliott Abrams

Gary Bauer

William J. Bennett

Jeb Bush

Dick Cheney

Eliot A. Cohen

Midge Decter

Paula Dobriansky

Steve Forbes

Aaron Friedberg

Francis Fukuyama

Frank Gaffney

Fred C. Iklé

Donald Kagan

Zalmay Khalilzad

I. Lewis Libby

Norman Podhoretz

Dan Quayle

Peter W. Rodman

Stephen P. Rosen

Henry S. Rowen

Donald Rumsfeld

Vin Weber

George Weigel

Paul Wolfowitz

Appendix B:
Address to the Nation by President George W. Bush, September 11, 2001

Good evening. Today, our fellow citizens, our way of life, our very freedom came under attack in a series of deliberate and deadly terrorist acts. The victims were in airplanes, or in their offices; secretaries, businessmen and women, military and federal workers; moms and dads, friends and neighbors. Thousands of lives were suddenly ended by evil, despicable acts of terror.

The pictures of airplanes flying into buildings, fires burning, huge structures collapsing have filled us with disbelief, terrible sadness, and a quiet, unyielding anger. These acts of mass murder were intended to frighten our nation into chaos and retreat. But they have failed; our country is strong.

A great people has been moved to defend a great nation. Terrorist attacks can shake the foundations of our biggest buildings, but they cannot touch the foundation of America. These acts shattered steel, but they cannot dent the steel of American resolve.

America was targeted for attack because we're the brightest beacon for freedom and opportunity in the world. And no one will keep that light from shining.

Today, our nation saw evil, the very worst of human nature. And we responded with the best of America—with the daring of our rescue workers, with the caring for strangers and neighbors who came to give blood and help in any way they could.

Immediately following the first attack, I implemented our government's emergency response plans. Our military is powerful, and it's prepared. Our emergency teams are working in New York City and Washington, DC, to help with local rescue efforts.

Our first priority is to get help to those who have been injured and to take every precaution to protect our citizens at home and around the world from further attacks.

The functions of our government continue without interruption. Federal agencies in Washington which had to be evacuated today are reopening for essential personnel tonight, and will be open for business tomorrow. Our financial institutions remain strong, and the American economy will be open for business, as well.

The search is under way for those who are behind these evil acts. I've directed the full resources of our intelligence and law enforcement communities to find those responsible and to bring them to justice. We will make no distinction between the terrorists who committed these acts and those who harbor them.

I appreciate so very much the members of Congress who have joined me in strongly condemning these attacks. And on behalf of the American people, I thank the many world leaders who have called to offer their condolences and assistance.

America and our friends and allies join with all those who want peace and security in the world, and we stand together to win the war against terrorism. Tonight, I ask for your prayers for all those who grieve, for the children whose worlds have been shattered, for all whose sense of safety and security has been threatened. And I pray they will be comforted by a power greater than any of us, spoken through the ages in Psalm 23: "Even though I walk through the valley of the shadow of death, I fear no evil, for You are with me."

This is a day when all Americans from every walk of life unite in our resolve for justice and peace. America has stood down enemies before, and we will do so this time. None of us will ever forget this day. Yet, we go forward to defend freedom and all that is good and just in our world.

Thank you. Good night, and God bless America.

Appendix C:
Article 3 of the Third Geneva Convention, on the Treatment of Prisoners of War

In the case of armed conflict not of an international character occurring in the territory of one of the High Contracting Parties, each Party to the conflict shall be bound to apply, as a minimum, the following provisions:

(1) Persons taking no active part in the hostilities, including members of armed forces who have laid down their arms and those placed hors de combat by sickness, wounds, detention, or any other cause, shall in all circumstances be treated humanely, without any adverse distinction founded on race, color, religion or faith, sex, birth or wealth, or any other similar criteria. To this end, the following acts are and shall remain prohibited at any time and in any place whatsoever with respect to the above-mentioned persons:

(a) violence to life and person, in particular murder of all kinds, mutilation, cruel treatment and torture;

(b) taking of hostages;

(c) outrages upon personal dignity, in particular humiliating and degrading treatment;

(d) the passing of sentences and the carrying out of executions without previous judgment pronounced by a regularly constituted court, affording all the judicial guarantees which are recognized as indispensable by civilized peoples.

(2) The wounded and sick shall be collected and cared for.

An impartial humanitarian body, such as the International Committee of the Red Cross, may offer its services to the Parties to the conflict. The Parties to the conflict should further endeavor to bring into force, by means of special agreements, all or part of the other provisions of the present Convention. The application of the preceding provisions shall not affect the legal status of the Parties to the conflict.

Appendix D:
Farewell Address to the Nation by President George W. Bush, January 15, 2009

Fellow citizens: For eight years, it has been my honor to serve as your president. The first decade of this new century has been a period of consequence—a time set apart. Tonight, with a thankful heart, I have asked for a final opportunity to share some thoughts on the journey that we have traveled together and the future of our nation.

Five days from now, the world will witness the vitality of American democracy. In a tradition dating back to our founding, the presidency will pass to a successor chosen by you, the American people. Standing on the steps of the Capitol will be a man whose history reflects the enduring promise of our land. This is a moment of hope and pride for our whole nation. And I join all Americans in offering best wishes to President-Elect Obama, his wife Michelle, and their two beautiful girls.

Tonight, I am filled with gratitude—to Vice President Cheney and members of my administration; to Laura, who brought joy to this house and love to my life; to our wonderful daughters, Barbara and Jenna; to my parents, whose examples have provided strength for a lifetime. And above all, I thank the American people for the trust you have given me. I thank you for the prayers that have lifted my spirits. And I thank you for the countless acts of courage, generosity, and grace that I have witnessed these past eight years.

This evening, my thoughts return to the first night I addressed you from this house—September the 11th, 2001. That morning, terrorists took nearly

3,000 lives in the worst attack on America since Pearl Harbor. I remember standing in the rubble of the World Trade Center three days later, surrounded by rescuers who had been working around the clock. I remember talking to brave souls who charged through smoke-filled corridors at the Pentagon and to husbands and wives whose loved ones became heroes aboard Flight 93. I remember Arlene Howard, who gave me her fallen son's police shield as a reminder of all that was lost. And I still carry his badge.

As the years passed, most Americans were able to return to life much as it had been before 9/11. But I never did. Every morning, I received a briefing on the threats to our nation. I vowed to do everything in my power to keep us safe.

Over the past seven years, a new Department of Homeland Security has been created. The military, the intelligence community, and the FBI have been transformed. Our nation is equipped with new tools to monitor the terrorists' movements, freeze their finances, and break up their plots. And with strong allies at our side, we have taken the fight to the terrorists and those who support them. Afghanistan has gone from a nation where the Taliban harbored al Qaeda and stoned women in the streets to a young democracy that is fighting terror and encouraging girls to go to school. Iraq has gone from a brutal dictatorship and a sworn enemy of America to an Arab democracy at the heart of the Middle East and a friend of the United States.

There is legitimate debate about many of these decisions. But there can be little debate about the results. America has gone more than seven years without another terrorist attack on our soil. This is a tribute to those who toil night and day to keep us safe—law enforcement officers, intelligence analysts, homeland security and diplomatic personnel, and the men and women of the United States Armed Forces.

Our nation is blessed to have citizens who volunteer to defend us in this time of danger. I have cherished meeting these selfless patriots and their families. And America owes you a debt of gratitude. And to all our men and women in uniform listening tonight: There has been no higher honor than serving as your commander-in-chief.

The battles waged by our troops are part of a broader struggle between two dramatically different systems. Under one, a small band of fanatics demands total obedience to an oppressive ideology, condemns women to subservience, and marks unbelievers for murder. The other system is based on the conviction that freedom is the universal gift of Almighty God and that liberty and justice light the path to peace.

This is the belief that gave birth to our nation. And in the long run, advancing this belief is the only practical way to protect our citizens. When people live in freedom, they do not willingly choose leaders who pursue campaigns of terror. When people have hope in the future, they will not cede their lives to violence and extremism. So around the world, America is promoting human liberty, human rights, and human dignity. We're standing with dissidents and young democracies, providing AIDS medicine to dying patients—to bring dying patients back to life, and sparing mothers and babies from malaria. And this great republic born alone in liberty is leading the world toward a new age when freedom belongs to all nations.

For eight years, we've also strived to expand opportunity and hope here at home. Across our country, students are rising to meet higher standards in public schools. A new Medicare prescription drug benefit is bringing peace of mind to seniors and the disabled. Every taxpayer pays lower income taxes. The addicted and suffering are finding new hope through faith-based programs. Vulnerable human life is better protected. Funding for our veterans has nearly doubled. America's air and water and lands are measurably cleaner. And the federal bench includes wise new members like Justice Sam Alito and Chief Justice John Roberts.

When challenges to our prosperity emerged, we rose to meet them. Facing the prospect of a financial collapse, we took decisive measures to safeguard our economy. These are very tough times for hardworking families, but the toll would be far worse if we had not acted. All Americans are in this together. And together, with determination and hard work, we will restore our economy to the path of growth. We will show the world once again the resilience of America's free enterprise system.

Like all who have held this office before me, I have experienced setbacks. There are things I would do differently if given the chance. Yet I've always acted with the best interests of our country in mind. I have followed my conscience and done what I thought was right. You may not agree with some of the tough decisions I have made. But I hope you can agree that I was willing to make the tough decisions.

The decades ahead will bring more hard choices for our country, and there are some guiding principles that should shape our course.

While our nation is safer than it was seven years ago, the gravest threat to our people remains another terrorist attack. Our enemies are patient and determined to strike again. America did nothing to seek or deserve this conflict. But we have been given solemn responsibilities, and we must meet them. We must resist complacency. We must keep our resolve. And we must never let down our guard.

At the same time, we must continue to engage the world with confidence and clear purpose. In the face of threats from abroad, it can be tempting to seek comfort by turning inward. But we must reject isolationism and its companion, protectionism. Retreating behind our borders would only invite danger. In the twenty-first century, security and prosperity at home depend on the expansion of liberty abroad. If America does not lead the cause of freedom, that cause will not be led.

As we address these challenges—and others we cannot foresee tonight—America must maintain our moral clarity. I've often spoken to you about good and evil, and this has made some uncomfortable. But good and evil are present in this world, and between the two of them there can be no compromise. Murdering the innocent to advance an ideology is wrong every time, everywhere. Freeing people from oppression and despair is eternally right. This nation must continue to speak out for justice and truth. We must always be willing to act in their defense—and to advance the cause of peace.

President Thomas Jefferson once wrote, "I like the dreams of the future better than the history of the past." As I leave the house he occupied two centuries ago, I share that optimism. America is a young country, full of vitality, constantly growing and renewing itself. And even in the toughest times, we lift our eyes to the broad horizon ahead.

I have confidence in the promise of America because I know the character of our people. This is a nation that inspires immigrants to risk everything for the dream of freedom. This is a nation where citizens show calm in times of danger and compassion in the face of suffering. We see examples of America's character all around us. And Laura and I have invited some of them to join us in the White House this evening.

We see America's character in Dr. Tony Recasner, a principal who opened a new charter school from the ruins of Hurricane Katrina. We see it in Julio Medina, a former inmate who leads a faith-based program to help prisoners returning to society. We've seen it in Staff Sergeant Aubrey McDade, who charged into an ambush in Iraq and rescued three of his fellow Marines.

We see America's character in Bill Krissoff—a surgeon from California. His son, Nathan—a Marine—gave his life in Iraq. When I met Dr. Krissoff and his family, he delivered some surprising news: He told me he wanted to join the Navy Medical Corps in honor of his son. This good man was 60 years old—18 years above the age limit. But his petition for a waiver was granted, and for the past year he has trained in battlefield medicine. Lieutenant Commander Krissoff could not be here tonight, because he will soon deploy to Iraq, where he will help save America's wounded warriors—and uphold the legacy of his fallen son.

In citizens like these, we see the best of our country—resilient and hopeful, caring and strong. These virtues give me an unshakable faith in America. We have faced danger and trial, and there's more ahead. But with the courage of our people and confidence in our ideals, this great nation will never tire, never falter, and never fail.

It has been the privilege of a lifetime to serve as your president. There have been good days and tough days. But every day I have been inspired by the greatness of our country and uplifted by the goodness of our people. I have been blessed to represent this nation we love. And I will always be honored to carry a title that means more to me than any other—citizen of the United States of America.

And so, my fellow Americans, for the final time: Good night. May God bless this house and our next president. And may God bless you and our wonderful country. Thank you.

Appendix E:
Barack Obama's Victory Speech, November 5, 2008

Hello, Chicago.

If there is anyone out there who still doubts that America is a place where all things are possible, who still wonders if the dream of our founders is alive in our time, who still questions the power of our democracy, tonight is your answer.

It's the answer told by lines that stretched around schools and churches in numbers this nation has never seen, by people who waited three hours and four hours, many for the first time in their lives, because they believed that this time must be different, that their voices could be that difference.

It's the answer spoken by young and old, rich and poor, Democrat and Republican, black, white, Hispanic, Asian, Native American, gay, straight, disabled and not disabled, Americans who sent a message to the world that we have never been just a collection of individuals or a collection of red states and blue states.

We are, and always will be, the United States of America.

It's the answer that led those who've been told for so long by so many to be cynical and fearful and doubtful about what we can achieve to put their hands on the arc of history and bend it once more toward the hope of a better day.

It's been a long time coming, but tonight, because of what we did on this date in this election at this defining moment, change has come to America.

A little bit earlier this evening, I received an extraordinarily gracious call from Senator McCain.

Senator McCain fought long and hard in this campaign. And he's fought even longer and harder for the country that he loves. He has endured sacrifices for America that most of us cannot begin to imagine. We are better off for the service rendered by this brave and selfless leader.

I congratulate him; I congratulate Governor Palin for all that they've achieved. And I look forward to working with them to renew this nation's promise in the months ahead.

I want to thank my partner in this journey, a man who campaigned from his heart and spoke for the men and women he grew up with on the streets of Scranton and rode with on the train home to Delaware, the vice president-elect of the United States, Joe Biden.

And I would not be standing here tonight without the unyielding support of my best friend for the last sixteen years, the rock of our family, the love of my life, the nation's next first lady, Michelle Obama.

Sasha and Malia, I love you both more than you can imagine. And you have earned the new puppy that's coming with us to the new White House.

And while she's no longer with us, I know my grandmother is watching, along with the family that made me who I am. I miss them tonight. I know that my debt to them is beyond measure.

To my sister Maya, my sister Alma, all my other brothers and sisters, thank you so much for all the support that you've given me. I am grateful to them.

And to my campaign manager, David Plouffe, the unsung hero of this campaign, who built the best—the best political campaign, I think, in the history of the United States of America.

To my chief strategist, David Axelrod, who has been a partner with me every step of the way. To the best campaign team ever assembled in the history of politics, you made this happen, and I am forever grateful for what you've sacrificed to get it done.

But above all, I will never forget who this victory truly belongs to. It belongs to you. It belongs to you.

I was never the likeliest candidate for this office. We didn't start with much money or many endorsements. Our campaign was not hatched in the halls of Washington. It began in the backyards of Des Moines and the living rooms of Concord and the front porches of Charleston. It was built by working men and women who dug into what little savings they had to give $5 and $10 and $20 to the cause.

It grew strength from the young people who rejected the myth of their generation's apathy, who left their homes and their families for jobs that offered little pay and less sleep.

It drew strength from the not-so-young people who braved the bitter cold and scorching heat to knock on doors of perfect strangers and from the millions of Americans who volunteered and organized and proved that more than two centuries later a government of the people, by the people, and for the people has not perished from the Earth.

This is your victory.

And I know you didn't do this just to win an election. And I know you didn't do it for me.

You did it because you understand the enormity of the task that lies ahead. For even as we celebrate tonight, we know the challenges that tomorrow will bring are the greatest of our lifetime—two wars, a planet in peril, the worst financial crisis in a century.

Even as we stand here tonight, we know there are brave Americans waking up in the deserts of Iraq and the mountains of Afghanistan to risk their lives for us.

There are mothers and fathers who will lie awake after the children fall asleep and wonder how they'll make the mortgage or pay their doctors' bills or save enough for their child's college education.

There's new energy to harness, new jobs to be created, new schools to build, and threats to meet, alliances to repair.

The road ahead will be long. Our climb will be steep. We may not get there in one year or even in one term. But, America, I have never been more hopeful than I am tonight that we will get there.

I promise you, we as a people will get there.

There will be setbacks and false starts. There are many who won't agree with every decision or policy I make as president. And we know the government can't solve every problem.

But I will always be honest with you about the challenges we face. I will listen to you, especially when we disagree. And, above all, I will ask you to join in the work of remaking this nation, the only way it's been done in America for 221 years—block by block, brick by brick, calloused hand by calloused hand.

What began 21 months ago in the depths of winter cannot end on this autumn night.

This victory alone is not the change we seek. It is only the chance for us to make that change. And that cannot happen if we go back to the way things were.

It can't happen without you, without a new spirit of service, a new spirit of sacrifice.

So let us summon a new spirit of patriotism, of responsibility, where each of us resolves to pitch in and work harder and look after not only ourselves but each other.

Let us remember that, if this financial crisis taught us anything, it's that we cannot have a thriving Wall Street while Main Street suffers.

In this country, we rise or fall as one nation, as one people. Let's resist the temptation to fall back on the same partisanship and pettiness and immaturity that has poisoned our politics for so long.

Let's remember that it was a man from this state who first carried the banner of the Republican Party to the White House, a party founded on the values of self-reliance and individual liberty and national unity.

Those are values that we all share. And while the Democratic Party has won a great victory tonight, we do so with a measure of humility and determination to heal the divides that have held back our progress.

As Lincoln said to a nation far more divided than ours, we are not enemies but friends. Though passion may have strained, it must not break our bonds of affection.

And to those Americans whose support I have yet to earn, I may not have won your vote tonight, but I hear your voices. I need your help. And I will be your president, too.

And to all those watching tonight from beyond our shores, from parliaments and palaces, to those who are huddled around radios in the forgotten corners of the world, our stories are singular, but our destiny is shared, and a new dawn of American leadership is at hand.

To those—to those who would tear the world down: We will defeat you. To those who seek peace and security: We support you. And to all those who have wondered if America's beacon still burns as bright: Tonight we proved once more that the true strength of our nation comes not from the might of our arms or the scale of our wealth, but from the enduring power of our ideals: democracy, liberty, opportunity, and unyielding hope.

That's the true genius of America: that America can change. Our union can be perfected. What we've already achieved gives us hope for what we can and must achieve tomorrow.

This election had many firsts and many stories that will be told for generations. But one that is on my mind tonight is about a woman who cast her ballot in Atlanta. She is a lot like the millions of others who stood in line to make their voice heard in this election except for one thing: Ann Nixon Cooper is 106 years old.

She was born just a generation past slavery; a time when there were no cars on the road or planes in the sky; when someone like her couldn't vote for two reasons—because she was a woman and because of the color of her skin.

And tonight, I think about all that she has seen throughout her century in America—the heartache and the hope; the struggle and the progress; the times we were told that we can't, and the people who pressed on with that American creed: Yes, we can.

At a time when women's voices were silenced and their hopes dismissed, she lived to see them stand up and speak out and reach for the ballot. Yes, we can.

When there was despair in the dust bowl and depression across the land, she saw a nation conquer fear itself with a New Deal, new jobs, a new sense of common purpose. Yes, we can.

When the bombs fell on our harbor and tyranny threatened the world, she was there to witness a generation rise to greatness and a democracy was saved. Yes, we can.

She was there for the buses in Montgomery, the hoses in Birmingham, a bridge in Selma, and a preacher from Atlanta who told a people that "we shall overcome." Yes, we can.

A man touched down on the moon, a wall came down in Berlin, a world was connected by our own science and imagination.

And this year, in this election, she touched her finger to a screen, and cast her vote, because after 106 years in America, through the best of times and the darkest of hours, she knows how America can change.

Yes, we can.

America, we have come so far. We have seen so much. But there is so much more to do. So tonight, let us ask ourselves—if our children should live to see the next century, if my daughters should be so lucky to live as long as Ann Nixon Cooper, what change will they see? What progress will we have made?

This is our chance to answer that call. This is our moment.

This is our time, to put our people back to work and open doors of opportunity for our kids; to restore prosperity and promote the cause of peace; to reclaim the American dream and reaffirm that fundamental truth, that, out of many, we are one; that while we breathe, we hope. And where we are met with cynicism and doubts and those who tell us that we can't, we will respond with that timeless creed that sums up the spirit of a people: Yes, we can.

Thank you. God bless you. And may God bless the United States of America.

Appendix F:
President Barack Obama's Inaugural Address,
January 20, 2009

My fellow citizens: I stand here today humbled by the task before us, grateful for the trust you've bestowed, mindful of the sacrifices borne by our ancestors.

I thank President Bush for his service to our nation as well as the generosity and cooperation he has shown throughout this transition.

Forty-four Americans have now taken the presidential oath. The words have been spoken during rising tides of prosperity and the still waters of peace. Yet, every so often, the oath is taken amidst gathering clouds and raging storms. At these moments, America has carried on not simply because of the skill or vision of those in high office, but because we, the people, have remained faithful to the ideals of our forebears and true to our founding documents.

So it has been; so it must be with this generation of Americans.

That we are in the midst of crisis is now well understood. Our nation is at war against a far-reaching network of violence and hatred. Our economy is badly weakened, a consequence of greed and irresponsibility on the part of some but also our collective failure to make hard choices and prepare the nation for a new age. Homes have been lost, jobs shed, businesses shuttered. Our health care is too costly, our schools fail too many— and each day brings further evidence that the ways we use energy strengthen our adversaries and threaten our planet.

These are the indicators of crisis, subject to data and statistics. Less measurable, but no less profound, is a sapping of confidence across our land, a nagging fear that America's decline is inevitable, that the next generation must lower its sights.

Today I say to you that the challenges we face are real. They are serious and they are many. They will not be met easily or in a short span of time. But know this America: They will be met.

On this day, we gather because we have chosen hope over fear, unity of purpose over conflict and discord. On this day, we come to proclaim an end to the petty grievances and false promises, the recriminations and worn-out dogmas that for far too long have strangled our politics. We remain a young nation. But in the words of Scripture, the time has come to set aside childish things. The time has come to reaffirm our enduring spirit; to choose our better history; to carry forward that precious gift, that noble idea passed on from generation to generation: the God-given promise that all are equal, all are free, and all deserve a chance to pursue their full measure of happiness.

In reaffirming the greatness of our nation we understand that greatness is never a given. It must be earned. Our journey has never been one of shortcuts or settling for less. It has not been the path for the faint-hearted, for those that prefer leisure over work or seek only the pleasures of riches and fame. Rather, it has been the risk-takers, the doers, the makers of things—some celebrated, but more often men and women obscure in their labor—who have carried us up the long rugged path towards prosperity and freedom.

For us, they packed up their few worldly possessions and traveled across oceans in search of a new life. For us, they toiled in sweatshops and settled the West, endured the lash of the whip and plowed the hard earth. For us, they fought and died in places like Concord and Gettysburg, Normandy and Khe Sahn.

Time and again these men and women struggled and sacrificed and worked till their hands were raw so that we might live a better life. They saw America as bigger than the sum of our individual ambitions, greater than all the differences of birth or wealth or faction.

This is the journey we continue today. We remain the most prosperous, powerful nation on Earth. Our workers are no less productive than when this crisis began. Our minds are no less inventive, our goods and services no less needed than they were last week or last month or last year. Our capacity remains undiminished. But our time of standing pat, of protecting narrow interests and putting off unpleasant decisions—that time has surely passed. Starting today, we must pick ourselves up, dust ourselves off, and begin again the work of remaking America.

For everywhere we look, there is work to be done. The state of our economy calls for action, bold and swift. And we will act, not only to create new jobs, but to lay a new foundation for growth. We will build the roads and bridges, the electric grids and digital lines that feed our commerce and bind us together. We'll restore science to its rightful place and wield technology's wonders to raise health care's quality and lower its cost. We will harness the sun and the winds and the soil to fuel our cars and run our factories. And we will transform our schools and colleges and universities to meet the demands of a new age. All this we can do. All this we will do.

Now, there are some who question the scale of our ambitions, who suggest that our system cannot tolerate too many big plans. Their memories are short, for they have forgotten what this country has already done, what free men and women can achieve when imagination is joined to common purpose and necessity to courage. What the cynics fail to understand is that the ground has shifted beneath them, that the stale political arguments that have consumed us for so long no longer apply.

The question we ask today is not whether our government is too big or too small, but whether it works—whether it helps families find jobs at a decent wage, care they can afford, a retirement that is dignified. Where the answer is yes, we intend to move forward. Where the answer is no, programs will end. And those of us who manage the public's dollars will be held to account, to spend wisely, reform bad habits, and do our business in the light of day, because only then can we restore the vital trust between a people and their government.

Nor is the question before us whether the market is a force for good or ill. Its power to generate wealth and expand freedom is unmatched. But this crisis has reminded us that without a watchful eye, the market can spin out of control. The nation cannot prosper long when it favors only the prosperous. The success of our economy has always depended not just on the size of our gross domestic product, but on the reach of our prosperity, on the ability to extend opportunity to every willing heart—not out of charity, but because it is the surest route to our common good.

As for our common defense, we reject as false the choice between our safety and our ideals. Our Founding Fathers—our Founding Fathers—faced with perils that we can scarcely imagine, drafted a charter to assure the rule of law and the rights of man—a charter expanded by the blood of generations. Those ideals still light the world, and we will not give them up for expedience sake.

And so, to all the other peoples and governments who are watching today, from the grandest capitals to the small village where my father was born, know that America is a friend of each nation, and every man, woman, and child who seeks a future of peace and dignity. And we are ready to lead once more.

Recall that earlier generations faced down fascism and communism not just with missiles and tanks, but with the sturdy alliances and enduring convictions. They understood that our power alone cannot protect us, nor does it entitle us to do as we please. Instead they knew that our power grows through its prudent use; our security emanates from the justness of our cause, the force of our example, the tempering qualities of humility and restraint.

We are the keepers of this legacy. Guided by these principles once more, we can meet those new threats that demand even greater effort, even greater cooperation and understanding between nations. We will begin to responsibly leave Iraq to its people and forge a hard-earned peace in Afghanistan. With old friends and former foes, we'll work tirelessly to lessen the nuclear threat and roll back the specter of a warming planet.

We will not apologize for our way of life, nor will we waver in its defense. And for those who seek to advance their aims by inducing terror and slaughtering innocents, we say to you now that our spirit is stronger and cannot be broken—you cannot outlast us, and we will defeat you.

For we know that our patchwork heritage is a strength, not a weakness. We are a nation of Christians and Muslims, Jews and Hindus, and nonbelievers. We are shaped by every language and culture, drawn from every end of this Earth, and because we have tasted the bitter swill of civil war and segregation, and emerged from that dark chapter stronger and more united, we cannot help but believe that the old hatreds shall someday pass; that the lines of tribe shall soon dissolve; that, as the world grows smaller, our common humanity shall reveal itself; and that America must play its role in ushering in a new era of peace.

To the Muslim world, we seek a new way forward, based on mutual interest and mutual respect. To those leaders around the globe who seek to sow conflict or blame their society's ills on the West, know that your people will judge you on what you can build, not what you destroy.

To those who cling to power through corruption and deceit and the silencing of dissent, know that you are on the wrong side of history, but that we will extend a hand if you are willing to unclench your fist.

To the people of poor nations, we pledge to work alongside you to make your farms flourish and let clean waters flow, to nourish starved bodies and feed hungry minds. And to those nations like ours that enjoy relative plenty, we say we can no longer afford indifference to the suffering outside our borders, nor can we consume the world's resources without regard to effect. For the world has changed, and we must change with it.

As we consider the role that unfolds before us, we remember with humble gratitude those brave Americans who at this very hour patrol far-off deserts and distant mountains. They have something to tell us, just as the fallen heroes who lie in Arlington whisper through the ages.

We honor them not only because they are the guardians of our liberty, but because they embody the spirit of service—a willingness to find meaning in something greater than themselves.

And yet at this moment, a moment that will define a generation, it is precisely this spirit that must inhabit us all. For as much as government can do, and must do, it is ultimately the faith and determination of the American people upon which this nation relies. It is the kindness to take in a stranger when the levees break, the selflessness of workers who would rather cut their hours than see a friend lose their job which sees us through our darkest hours. It is the firefighter's courage to storm a stairway filled with smoke, but also a parent's willingness to nurture a child that finally decides our fate.

Our challenges may be new. The instruments with which we meet them may be new. But those values upon which our success depends—honesty and hard work, courage and fair play, tolerance and curiosity, loyalty and patriotism—these things are old. These things are true. They have been the quiet force of progress throughout our history.

What is demanded, then, is a return to these truths. What is required of us now is a new era of responsibility—a recognition on the part of every American that we have duties to ourselves, our nation, and the world; duties that we do not grudgingly accept but rather seize gladly, firm in the knowledge that there is nothing so satisfying to the spirit, so defining of our character than giving our all to a difficult task.

This is the price and the promise of citizenship. This is the source of our confidence—the knowledge that God calls on us to shape an uncertain destiny. This is the meaning of our liberty and our creed, why men and women and children of every race and every faith can join in celebration across this magnificent mall, and why a man whose father less than sixty years ago might not have been served in a local restaurant can now stand before you to take a most sacred oath.

So let us mark this day with remembrance of who we are and how far we have traveled. In the year of America's birth, in the coldest of months, a small band of patriots huddled by dying campfires on the shores of an icy river. The capital was abandoned. The enemy was advancing. The snow was stained with blood. At the moment when the outcome of our revolution was most in doubt, the father of our nation ordered these words to be read to the people: "Let it be told to the future world . . . that in the depth of winter, when nothing but hope and virtue could survive . . . that the city and the country, alarmed at one common danger, came forth to meet [it]."

America, in the face of our common dangers, in this winter of our hardship, let us remember these timeless words. With hope and virtue, let us brave once more the icy currents, and endure what storms may come. Let it be said by our children's children that when we were tested we refused to let this journey end, that we did not turn back nor did we falter, and with eyes fixed on the horizon and God's grace upon us, we carried forth that great gift of freedom and delivered it safely to future generations.

Thank you. God bless you. And God bless the United States of America.

Notes

Prologue

1. Professor Marc W. Herold, "A Dossier on Civilian Victims of United States' Aerial Bombing of Afghanistan: A Comprehensive Accounting (Revised)," March 2002, http://www.cursor.org/stories/civilian_deaths.htm.
2. According to the CIA World Factbook, daily oil consumption in the United States was 19.5 million barrels (2008 estimate), in China 7.85 million (2007 estimate), and in India 2.94 million barrels (2008 estimate) (https://www.cia.gov/library/publications/the-world-factbook/rankorder/2174rank.html). Data is frequently revised.
3. Graham Paterson, "Alan Greenspan Claims Iraq War Was Really for Oil," *Times*, September 16, 2007.
4. Nafeez Mossadeq Ahmed, "Ex-British Army Chief Confirms Peak Oil Motive for War," *Atlantic Free Press*, June 18, 2008.
5. Walter Pincus and Dana Milbank, "Al-Qaeda-Hussein Link Is Dismissed," *Washington Post*, June 17, 2004.
6. American Civil Liberties Union, "Why a Surveillance Society Clock?" http://www.aclu.org/privacy/spying/31543res20070904.html.

Chapter 1. Anatomy of Neoconservatism

1. See Federal Election Commission, "2000 Official Presidential General Election Results," December 2001, http://www.fec.gov/pubrec/2000presgeresults.htm; and CNN, "How We Got Here: A Timeline of the Florida Recount," December 13, 2000, http://archives.cnn.com/2000/ALLPOLITICS/stories/12/13/got.here/index.html.
2. *Election 2000: The Role of the Courts, the Role of the Media, the Role of the Dice*, Conference Report (Evanston, IL: Northwestern University School of Law, January 2001).
3. John Harris, "Cheney Calls Kerry Unfit," *Washington Post*, September 2, 2004.
4. Democratic National Convention Committee, *2004 Democratic National Platform for America*, Washington, DC, July 27, 2004.
5. Brandon Crocker, "Thick Hair, but Thin Skin," *American Spectator Online*, September 8, 2004, http://spectator.org/archives/2004/09/08/thick-hair-but-thin-skin.

6. Owen Bennett-Jones, interview with Kofi Annan, BBC World Service, September 16, 2004.

7. For example, Dick Cheney, Donald Rumsfeld, Paul Wolfowitz, Zalmay Khalilzad, and Fred Iklé. Jeb Bush, the younger brother of George W. Bush and later the governor of Florida, was also among the founders.

8. Bill Clinton's affair with White House intern Monica Lewinsky; controversy over Bill and Hillary Clinton's business dealings with Whitewater Corporation, a real estate company that later failed, in the 1970s and 1980s.

9. This quotation and all others in this section are from "Statement of Principles" (Washington, DC: Project for the New American Century, June 3, 1997).

10. "Religion and the Presidential Vote" (Washington, DC: Pew Research Center for the People and the Press, December 6, 2004).

11. Maralee Schwartz and Kenneth J. Cooper, "Equal Rights Initiative in Iowa Attacked," *Washington Post*, August 23, 1992.

12. Pat Robertson, *700 Club*, ABC Family, June 8, 1998.

13. *Radio Factor with Bill O'Reilly*, June 17, 2004.

14. Many commentators have made this point about the Bush presidency, but here I acknowledge the comment made by David Remes, a lawyer for a group of Guantánamo detainees, quoted in Charles Babington and Michael Abramowitz, "U.S. Shifts Policy on Geneva Conventions," *Washington Post*, July 12, 2006.

15. Rumsfeld resigned as defense secretary in November 2006 amid acrimony over the conduct of the war on terror. The deputy defense secretary, Paul Wolfowitz, left to become president of the World Bank in June 2005; he was forced to resign after controversy over his role in the decisions about pay and promotions for his partner, Shaha Riza, a World Bank employee. John Bolton resigned as American ambassador to the UN in December 2006 after it became clear the Senate would not confirm him.

16. Paul Wolfowitz, interview in the *San Francisco Chronicle*, February 23, 2002; transcript, U.S. Department of Defense, Washington, DC.

17. Irving Kristol, "The Neoconservative Persuasion," *Weekly Standard*, August 25, 2003, http://www.weeklystandard.com/Utilities/printer_preview.asp?idArticle=3000&R=7 85F27881.

18. George W. Bush, State of the Union address (Washington, DC, January 31, 2006).

19. See Ian Rutledge, *Addicted to Oil: America's Relentless Drive for Energy Security* (London: I. B. Tauris, 2006).

20. Rutledge specially mentions British prime minister Tony Blair, a staunch ally of President Bush in the war on terror. See ibid., xix, 122, http://www.oiladdict.com/about.asp.

21. The forty-six-page document written by Wolfowitz was leaked to the *New York Times*. It generated controversy, after which the White House announced that Wolfowitz's boss, Dick Cheney, then defense secretary, would rewrite the draft. For key points in the Wolfowitz document, see "Excerpts from 1992 Draft 'Defense Planning Guidance,'" *Frontline: The War Behind Closed Doors*, PBS, February 20, 2003, http://www.pbs.org/wgbh/pages/frontline/shows/iraq/etc/wolf.html.

22. Kristol, "Neoconservative Persuasion."

23. Richard Viguerie, "Bush White House Hides True Scope of Federal Deficit," *Free Press*, August 1, 2008, http://www.freepress.org/departments/display/20/2008/3171.

24. Joseph Stiglitz, "War Costs and Costs and Costs," *Guardian Comment*, March 13, 2008, http://www.guardian.co.uk/commentisfree/2008/mar/13/warcostsandcostsandcosts.

25. Donald Rumsfeld, "Talking Points: National Security Policy Issues—Post–Cold War Threats," memorandum, in "Early Notions of Pre-Emption," The Bush Files, comp. Paul O'Neill. The Bush Files were published by Ron Suskind in *The Price of Loyalty* (New York: Simon & Schuster, 2004) and are available at http://thepriceofloyalty.ronsuskind.com/thebushfiles/.
26. The Oklahoma City bombers were Timothy McVeigh, who was executed, and Terry Nichols, who received a life sentence. Michael Fortier, who testified against McVeigh and Nichols, was sentenced to twelve years in prison for failing to warn the authorities.
27. Mark Sobel, "Briefing for NSC Principals on Gulf Policy," memorandum to Paul O'Neill, January 31, 2001. The purpose of the briefing, to be held the following day, was "to review the state of play, including a CIA briefing on Iraq, and to examine how to proceed." See "First Week's Plans for Iraqi Takeover," Bush Files.
28. National Security Council (NSC), *The National Security Strategy of the United States of America* (Washington, DC: September 2002), 1–2.
29. Lawrence Cumins, *Iraq Oil: Reserves, Production and Potential Revenues* (Washington, DC: Congressional Research Service, April 13, 2005), 1.
30. Paterson, "Alan Greenspan Claims."

Chapter 2. With Us or Without Us
1. George W. Bush, "Remarks by the President after Two Planes Crash into World Trade Center 9:30 A.M. EDT, September 11, 2001," in *September 11, 2001: Attack on America*, the Avalon Project, Yale Law School, New Haven, CT.
2. George W. Bush, "Statement by the President in His Address to the Nation 8:30 P.M. EDT, September 11, 2001," in ibid.
3. George W. Bush, "Remarks by President Bush to Employees of the Pentagon 11:45 A.M. EDT, September 17, 2001," in ibid.
4. George W. Bush, "Remarks by the President with the National Security Team 10:53 A.M. EDT, September 12, 2001"; and "Address to a Joint Session of Congress and the American People (as Delivered Before Congress) 9:00 P.M. EDT, September 20, 2001," in ibid. Also see George W. Bush, "Remarks by the President to United Nations General Assembly 9:38 A.M. EST, November 10, 2001," in ibid.
5. In 1992 the U.S. budget deficit was a record $290 billion after years spent running a war economy. For an assessment of Clinton's economic agenda, see John Dumbrell, *American Foreign Policy: Carter to Clinton* (London: Macmillan, 1997), 189–92.
6. See Gary Sick, "The Bush Doctrine: Imperial Moment," *World Today*, December 2002, 4–6.
7. George W. Bush, "The President's State of the Union Address, January 29, 2002," in *September 11, 2001*, The Avalon Project.
8. Only three countries—Pakistan, Saudi Arabia, and the United Arab Emirates—recognized the Taliban regime, which did not occupy Afghanistan's seat in the United Nations.
9. NSC, *National Security Strategy*.
10. Ibid., 30.
11. See Paul Rogers, "Unilateralism: Right for America, Right for the World," *World Today*, February 2002, 13–14.
12. George W. Bush and Jacques Chirac, "President Says Coalition Partners 'Must Perform' 11:44 A.M. EST, November 6, 2001," in *September 11, 2001*, The Avalon Project.

NOTES

13. Adam Wolfson, "Between Idealism and Realism," *Claremont Review of Books*, Summer 2005, http://www.claremont.org/publications/crb/id.1102/article_detail.asp; Robert Nolan, *Bush II: Balancing Realism and Idealism* (New York: Foreign Policy Association, January 20, 2005, http://www.fpa.org/newsletter_info2583/newsletter_info_sub_list.htm?section=Bush%20II%3A%20A%20return%20to%20realism%3F); William Safire, "Realism," *New York Times Magazine*, December 24, 2006, http://www.nytimes.com/2006/12/24/magazine/24wwln_safire.t.html.

14. Michael J. Mazarr describes it as "incomplete idealism." See his article "George W Bush, Idealist," *International Affairs*, May 2003, 503–22.

15. George W. Bush, "State of the Union Address" (Washington, DC, January 28, 2008). See also Bush's State of the Union addresses on January 23, 2007, January 31, 2006, and February 2, 2005.

16. Pervez Musharraf, "Statement by the President of Pakistan, September 12, 2001," in *September 11, 2001*, The Avalon Project.

17. For a look at the historical development of Pakistan, see Hussain Haqqani, *Pakistan: Between Mosque and Military* (Washington, DC: Carnegie Endowment for International Peace, 2005).

18. George W. Bush, Colin Powell, and John Ashcroft, "Remarks by the President, Secretary of State Colin Powell, and Attorney General John Ashcroft 9:19 A.M. EDT Camp David, September 15, 2001," in *September 11, 2001*, The Avalon Project.

19. Pervez Musharraf, Pakistani national broadcast, September 19, 2001; see "Text: Pakistan President Musharraf," http://www.washingtonpost.com/wp-srv/nation/specials/attacked/transcripts/pakistantext_091901.html.

20. In the end, Pakistan carried our a series of nuclear tests in May 1998, two weeks after India had conducted its own test. India carried out its first nuclear explosion in 1974. See "Pakistan Nuclear Weapons: A Brief History of Pakistan's Nuclear Program," Federation of American Scientists, http://www.fas.org/nuke/guide/pakistan/nuke/.

21. For an overview, see Haqqani, *Pakistan*, 1–50.

22. The wars were in 1947–48, 1965, and 1971. There have been other minor border conflicts.

23. See "Directorate for Inter-Services Intelligence (ISI)," GlobalSecurity.Org, http://www.globalsecurity.org/intell/world/pakistan/isi.htm.

24. Yvonne Roberts, "Military Spending," *Guardian Unlimited*, November 13, 2007.

25. See Ayesha Siddiqa, "Pakistan's Permanent Crisis," *openDemocracy*, May 15, 2007, http://www.opendemocracy.net/conflict-india_pakistan/pakistan_crisis_4622.jsp. An independent political and defense analyst, Siddiqa is the author of an authoritative study, *Military Inc: Inside Pakistan's Military Economy* (London: Pluto Press, 2007).

26. SEATO members included Australia, New Zealand, the Philippines, Thailand, France, Britain, the United States, and Pakistan. Pakistan left the organization after its defeat in the 1971 war with India. SEATO was dissolved in 1977. CENTO included Pakistan, Iran, Iraq, Turkey, and the United Kingdom. The organization became inactive in 1974, when Turkey invaded Cyprus. CENTO was disbanded after Pakistan, Turkey, and Iran withdrew from the organization following the fall of the Iranian monarchy in 1979.

27. Alan Kronstadt, *Pakistan-US Relations* (Washington, DC: Congressional Research Service, January 11, 2008).

28. Ibid., 17–18.

29. General Musharraf overthrew the elected government of Nawaz Sharif on October 12, 1999.

30. See "Pakistan," *2001 CIA World Factbook* (Washington, DC: Central Intelligence Agency, 2001, https://www.cia.gov/library/publications/download/download-2001/index.html.

31. *Terrorism Havens: Pakistan* (New York: Council on Foreign Relations, 2005).

32. Barry Buzan, "Will the Global War on Terrorism Be the New Cold War?" *International Affairs* 82, no. 6 (November 2006): 1102.

33. As in the killing of Brazilian national Jean Charles de Menezes by police officers in London on July 22, 2005.

34. Gareth Crossman, *Overlooked: Surveillance and Personal Privacy in Modern Britain*, with Hilary Kitchin, Rekha Kuna, Michael Skrein, and Jago Russell (London: Liberty/Nuffield Foundation, 2007), 20–34; "MP Was Bugged Twice, Report Says," BBC News, February 21, 2008; and Gordon Corera, "Who Watches the Watchers?" BBC News, February 6, 2008. For espionage on individual citizens, see, for example, American Civil Liberties Union, "Fact Sheet on the Police America Act," 2007, http://www.aclu.org/safefree/nsaspying/31203res20070807.html.

35. George W. Bush, remarks at a press conference with British prime minister Tony Blair, Washington, DC, July 17, 2003.

Chapter 3. Battle for Afghanistan

1. "Attacks Draw Mixed Response in Mideast," CNN, September 12, 2001.

2. UN Security Council, Resolution 1368, 2001.

3. UN General Assembly, First Resolution of the 56th UN General Assembly, 2001.

4. For example, Associated Press, "Bin Laden Denies Being Behind Attacks," September 16, 2001, quoting Al Jazeera TV News.

5. "In Full: Al-Qaeda Statement," BBC News, October 10, 2001, http://news.bbc.co.uk/1/low/world/middle_east/1590350.stm.

6. Al Jazeera refused to broadcast the interview, but CNN, which had an agreement with Al Jazeera, aired it in January 2002. See "Transcript of bin Laden's October Interview," CNN, February 5, 2002, http://archives.cnn.com/2002/WORLD/asiapcf/south/02/05/binladen.transcript/index.html. Also see David Bamber, "Bin Laden: Yes, I Did It," *Daily Telegraph*, November 11, 2001.

7. "Responsibility for the Terrorist Atrocities in the United States, September 11, 2001—An Updated Account," Ten Downing Street, October 4, 2001, http://www.fas.org/irp/news/2001/10/ukreport.html.

8. George W. Bush and Tony Blair, "Remarks by the President and Prime Minister of United Kingdom Tony Blair 8:12 P.M. EDT, September 20, 2001," in *September 11, 2001*, The Avalon Project.

9. For Tony Blair's admission that his religious faith guides his politics, see Kamal Ahmed, "Unease as Blair Lays Soul Bare," *Observer*, May 4, 2003.

10. "Bush Routinely Ignoring Blair," BBC News, November 30, 2006.

11. In October 2005, as a general election approached in Italy, Berlusconi said he had tried to persuade President Bush not to invade Iraq from the beginning. See Peter Popham, "Berlusconi: I Tried to Talk Bush Out of Invading Iraq," *Independent*, October 31, 2005.

12.   George W. Bush and José María Aznar, "Remarks by President Bush and Prime Minister Aznar of Spain in Photo Opportunity 11:55 A.M. EST, November 28, 2001," in *September 11, 2001*, The Avalon Project.

13.   Nuria del Viso, trans., "Spain: A Growing Commitment Towards Afghanistan," in *Elections in Afghanistan*, e-bulletin InfoCIP no. 5 (September 21, 2005).

14.   Jim Lobe, "Bush Terror War Suffers Body Blow in Spain," Inter Press Service, March 15, 2004, http://www.globalissues.org/article/471/bush-terror-war-suffers-body-blow-in-spain.

15.   Subsequent investigations and trial found that Basque separatists were not involved in the bombing. The bombing was carried out by a group of young men, mostly from North Africa, who, the prosecutors said, were inspired by al Qaeda.

16.   Aznar was referring to the Moorish occupation of Spain that began with an invasion from North Africa in 711. He was defending Pope Benedict XVI, who, quoting a Byzantine emperor, had said some teachings of the Prophet Mohammad were "evil and inhuman." The pope's remarks led to protests from Muslim groups. The pope later said he was deeply sorry.

17.   See Aznar: "Muslims Should Apologize for Occupying Spain for 800 Years," *Free Republic*, http://www.freerepublic.com/focus/f-news/1707057/posts. The initiative for negotiations with Muslim countries was launched by Spain's Socialist prime minister, José Luis Rodríguez Zapatero, who defeated Aznar's Popular Party in the 2004 general election. Zapatero's initiative was later adopted by the United Nations.

18.   ANZUS is a military alliance that binds Australia and New Zealand and, separately, the United States and Australia on defense matters in the Pacific region. For the decision to invoke ANZUS after 9/11, see Angus Martyn, "The Right of Self-Defense under International Law: The Response to the Terrorist Attacks of 11 September," in *Current Issues Brief* 8 (2001–2), http://www.aph.gov.au/library/pubs/CIB/2001-02/02cib08.htm#legal; and "Attacks Changed Our Lives," *The Age*, September 11, 2005, http://www.theage.com.au/news/opinion/attacks-changed-our-lives/2005/09/10/1125772729255.html.

19.   John Howard had been prime minister for thirteen years. The longest-serving Australian prime minister was Robert Menzies (December 1949–January 1966).

20.   Fifty-eight French soldiers died in a separate attack. The multinational force had been deployed after the 1982 Israeli invasion of Lebanon.

21.   Scott Baldauf, "Afghanistan's Lion of Panjshir," *Christian Science Monitor*, September 12, 2001, http://www.csmonitor.com/2001/0912/p6s1-wosc.html. For foreign support, see Agence France Presse, "Afghan Leader Pressures Europe over Taliban," *Omaid Weekly*, April 5, 2001, http://www.omaid.com/english_section/in_the_press/ASM_EU.htm.

22.   Rahul Bedi, "India Joins Anti-Taliban Coalition," *Jane's Intelligence Review*, March 15, 2001, http://www.janes.com/security/international_security/news/jir/jir010315_1_n.shtml; George Arney, "US Planned Attack on Taleban," BBC, September 18, 2001; Associated Press, "US Had Plan to Overthrow Taliban, March 23, 2004."

23.   Using B-1, B-2, and B-52 bombers, as well as Tomahawk cruise missiles. One reason for the high-altitude campaign was the fear that Taliban and al Qaeda fighters still had between two and three hundred heat-seeking Stinger missiles, supplied by America to the Afghan mujahideen during the proxy war against the Soviet Union in the 1980s. See Michael O'Hanlon, "A Flawed Masterpiece," *Foreign Affairs* 81, no. 3 (March–April 2002): 51.

24. Civilian casualties from October 7, 2001, to March 2002: 3,100–3,500 civilians killed directly by bombs and missiles; 4,000–6,500 injured; 4,000–6,000 dead Taliban and allies; an estimated minimum of 19,800 Afghan refugees dying of hunger, disease, and cold in camps; and an additional estimated 5,000 war widows and thousands of orphans. See Marc W. Herold, "US Bombing and Afghan Civilian Deaths—Official Neglect of 'Unworthy' Bodies," *International Journal of Urban and Regional Research* 26, no. 3 (September 2002): 626–34.

25. O'Hanlon, "Flawed Masterpiece," 51. At times, O'Hanlon seems overzealous in describing the short-term success of the war to overthrow the Taliban regime (October–December 2001), and his narrative should therefore be taken with caution.

26. See "From DEBKA Intelligence Files: The Phone Call Heard 'Round the World," *WorldNetDaily.com*, November 16, 2001, http://www.worldnetdaily.com/news/article.asp?ARTICLE_ID=25351.

27. Ibid.

28. "World Report 2002: Afghanistan," Human Rights Watch, http://hrw.org/wr2k2/asia1.html.

29. See Brian Whitaker, "Halt War, Says Ayatollah," *Guardian*, October 16, 2001. Also "Violent Protests Continue Across Muslim World," *Guardian*, October 12, 2001; Matthew Engel, "Muslim Allies Break Ranks with US," *Guardian*, October 16, 2001; "Indian Muslim Leader Warns of Protests," BBC, September 17, 2001; and "Protests Spread in Muslim Asia," CNN, September 21, 2001.

30. "Kabul Besieged by Northern Alliance," *Guardian*, November 12, 2001; "Taleban Routed Outside Kabul," BBC News Online, November 12, 2001, http://news.bbc.co.uk/2/low/south_asia/1651796.stm.

31. Donald Rumsfeld, "DoD News Briefing: Secretary Rumsfeld and Gen. Myers 2:31 P.M. EST, November 13, 2001," in *September 11, 2001*, The Avalon Project.

32. The troops went to Operation Enduring Freedom (the official name of one of the military campaigns in the war on terror) and the International Security Assistance Force in Kabul (established under the UN Security Council Resolution 1386 on December 20, 2001). See U.S. Department of Defense, "Fact Sheet," February 26, 2002.

Chapter 4. In Afghanistan, War Is Peace

1. The essay became the basis of his book *Of Paradise and Power* (New York: Knopf, 2003).

2. Robert Kagan, "Power and Weakness," *Policy Review*, no. 113 (June–July 2002), http://www.atlanticcommunity.org/Power%20and%20Weakness%20-%20Policy%20Review,%20No_%20113.htm.

3. For U.S. casualties in Vietnam, see Theodore J. Hull, "Statistical Information about Casualties of the Vietnam War," National Archive, February 2007, http://www.archives.gov/research/vietnam-war/casualty-statistics.html. For Soviet casualties in Afghanistan, see Russian General Staff, *The Soviet-Afghan War: How a Superpower Fought and Lost*, trans. and ed. Lester Grau and Michael Gress (Lawrence: University Press of Kansas, 2002), 43–44. Various accounts put the number of Soviet wounded in Afghanistan at more than 300,000.

4. See, for example, Rear Adm. John Stufflebeem, "Enduring Freedom Operation Update—Rear Adm. Stufflebeem 2 P.M. EST, November 14, 2001," in *September 11, 2001: Attack on America*, The Avalon Project, Yale Law School, New Haven, CT.

5. "US Is Said to Be Relying on ISI for Intelligence in Afghan War," Center for Grass-roots Oversight, November 3, 2001, http://www.historycommons.org/context.jsp?item=a110301usreliesonisi&scale=0#a110301usreliesonisi quoting Knight Ridder article of the same day.

6. Rod Nordland, Sami Yousafzai, and Babak Dehghanpisheh, "How Al-Qaeda Slipped Away," *Newsweek*, August 11, 2002.

7. Philip Smucker, "How Bin Laden Got Away," *Christian Science Monitor*, March 4, 2002.

8. Michael Scheuer, interview with *Frontline*, PBS, January 11, 2006.

9. Cyrus Hodes and Mark Sedra, *The Search for Security in Post-Taliban Afghanistan*, Adelphi Paper 391 (London: International Institute of Strategic Studies/Routledge, 2007), 19.

10. Seymour Hersh, "The Getaway," *The New Yorker*, January 28, 2002, http://www.newyorker.com/archive/2002/01/28/020128fa_FACT.

11. For data on Pakistani public opinion of the Taliban, see *Islamic Extremism: Common Concern for Muslim and Western Publics: Summary of Findings*, Pew Global Attitudes Project, July 14, 2005, http://pewglobal.org/reports/display.php?ReportID=248. Musharraf's dilemma is obvious to those interested in Pakistan, but Shaun Gregory articulates it succinctly. See *The ISI and the War on Terrorism* (Bradford, UK: Pakistan Security Research Unit, Department of Peace Studies, University of Bradford, January 24, 2008), 9.

12. For a list, see Gregory, *ISI and the War on Terrorism*, 10.

13. A series of confessions by Sheikh Mohammed were revealed in the text of an "informal military hearing" at the Guantánamo Bay detention camp made public in March 2007. See "Verbatim Transcript of Combatant Status Review Tribunal Hearing for ISN 10024," March 10, 2007, http://www.defenselink.mil/news/transcript_ISN10024.pdf; and Adam Liptak, "Terror Suspect Said to Confess to Other Acts," *New York Times*, March 15, 2007. Human Rights Watch, as well as Sheikh Mohammed, said that he was tortured in custody, and it was revealed that one of the techniques used on him was waterboarding.

14. House of Commons, *Report of the Official Account of Bombings in London on July 7, 2005* (London: Stationery Office, 2006); and *Intelligence and Security Committee Report on the London Terrorist Attacks on July 7, 2005* (London: Stationery Office, 2005).

15. See House of Commons, *Report of the Official Account of Bombings in London*, 26–27; and *Intelligence and Security Committee Report on the London Terrorist Attacks*, 12.

16. Hodes and Sedra, *Search for Security in Post-Taliban Afghanistan*, 30–31.

17. Mohammad Yousaf and Mark Adkin, *Afghanistan: The Bear Trap* (Barnsley, UK: Leo Cooper, 2001), 97–112.

18. See Frédéric Grare, "Pakistan: The Myth of an Islamist Peril," Policy Brief 45 (Washington, DC: Carnegie Endowment for International Peace, February 2006).

19. Zia-ul-Haq's reign ended abruptly in August 1988, when he died in a mysterious airplane crash.

20. For an analysis, see "Volatile Pakistan: Future in the Balance," *Strategic Comments* 13, no. 8 (October 2007), 1-2.

21. The Seventeenth Amendment passed in December 2003. For details, see "Constitution (Seventeenth Amendment) Act, 2003," http://www.pakistani.org/pakistan/constitution/amendments/17amendment.html.

22. See, for example, Ali Khan, "The Lawyers' Movement in Pakistan," *Jurist*, May–December 2007, 1-16; Salman Raja, "Pakistan: Inside the Storm," *openDemocracy*, November 9, 2007, http://www.opendemocracy.net/article/conflicts/pakistan_inside_the_storm; Bruce Loudon, "Pakistan Courts Frozen by Lawyers' Boycott," *The Australian*, December 7, 2007; Ali Dayan Hasan, "Pakistan's Future Imperfect," *Guardian Comment*, December 21, 2007.

23. "Volatile Pakistan," 3.

24. Selig S. Harrison, "Pakistan's Baluch Insurgency," *Le Monde Diplomatique*, October 2006, http://mondediplo.com/2006/10/05baluchistan.

25. "Unrest After Pakistan Rebel Death," *BBC*, August 27, 2006; and Nicholas Schmidle, "Waiting for the Worst: Baluchistan 2006," *Virginia Quarterly Review*, Spring 2007, http://www.vqronline.org/articles/2007/spring/schmidle-waiting-for-worst/.

26. Barnett Rubin and Abubakar Siddiqui, *Resolving the Pakistan-Afghanistan Stalemate*, Special Report (Washington, DC: U.S. Institute of Peace, October 2006), 11.

27. Annex I: International Security Force, in "The Bonn Agreement," 2001.

28. Alan Sipress, "Peacekeepers Won't Go Beyond Kabul, Cheney Says," *Washington Post*, March 20, 2002; William Maley, *Rescuing Afghanistan* (Sydney: University of New South Wales Press, 2006), 65; and William Maley, comments made in "Threats to Afghanistan's Transition" (conference at the Carnegie Endowment for International Peace, Washington, DC, May 8, 2007).

29. UN Resolution 1510, October 13, 2003.

30. Patricia Gossman, "Afghanistan: A Government of Warlords Threatens Kabul," *International Herald Tribune*, October 16, 2003.

31. For example, Uzbek warlord Abdul Rashid Dostum; Tajik militia leader Ismail Khan and his arch rival Amanullah Khan; Pashtun warlord Hazrat Ali, whose power base had been Jalalabad in Nangarhar Province in the east; and Kabul-born Abdul Rabb al-Rasul Sayyaf, a fundamentalist ex-mujahideen leader with close links to Saudi Wahhabis.

32. Esther Pan, *Afghanistan: Karzai versus the Warlords*, Council on Foreign Relations, September 15, 2004, http://www.cfr.org/publication/7791/afghanistan.html.

33. *Afghanistan Opium Survey 2007* (Vienna: United Nations Office on Drugs and Crime, October 2007), 7.

34. There are many books and articles on the Taliban resurgence, among them Antonio Giustozzi, *Koran, Kalashnikov, and Laptop: The Neo-Taliban Insurgency in Afghanistan, 2002–7* (New York: Columbia University Press, 2008); Thomas Johnson, "On the Edge of the Big Muddy: The Taliban Resurgence in Afghanistan," *China and Eurasia Forum Quarterly* 5, no. 2 (2007): 93–129; Shaun Gregory, "Al-Qaeda in Pakistan," Brief no. 5 (Bradford, UK: Pakistan Security Research Unit, Department of Peace Studies, University of Bradford, March 2007); and Hodes and Sedra, *Search for Security in Post-Taliban Afghanistan*, 17–32.

35. For a UN perspective on suicide attacks, see *Suicide Attacks in Afghanistan (2001–2007)* (Kabul: UN Assistance Mission to Afghanistan, September 1, 2007).

36. The full quote is "War Is Peace, Freedom Is Slavery, Ignorance Is Strength."

Chapter 5. Explaining the Invasion of Iraq

1. For the text of Christopher Meyer's letter to the British Prime Minister's Office, see "Iraq, Tony and the Truth: Timeline," BBC News, April 29, 2005.

2. The UN inspection regime was imposed on Iraq as part of the cease-fire agreement after the 1991 Gulf War for the liberation of Kuwait. It provided for (1) declaration by Iraq of its program of weapons of mass destruction and long-range missiles, (2) verification through the UN inspectors and the International Atomic Energy Agency, and (3) elimination of proscribed programs or items under the supervision of the two organizations.

3. The United States and Britain did launch missile attacks on Iraq in December 1998.

4. See "Iraq's Weapons of Mass Destruction: The Assessment of the British Government" (London: 10 Downing Street, September 24, 2002), 17.

5. Hans Blix, interview with *Independent*, March 5, 2004. Blix said the advice of Attorney General Lord Goldsmith to the British government giving cover for the invasion by America and Britain had no lawful justification. Blix said it would have required a second UN resolution explicitly authorizing the use of force for the invasion of Iraq to have been legal. In the same newspaper article, Cabinet Secretary Sir Andrew Turnbull revealed that the British government had assumed, until the eve of war, that it needed a specific UN mandate to authorize military action.

6. "Iraq War Illegal, Says Annan," BBC News, September 16, 2004,

7. CNN's security correspondent, John King, has collected detailed information, supported by documents, on how America armed Iraq in the 1980s. See his essay, "Arming Iraq and the Path to War," March 31, 2003, http://www.ratical.org/ratville/CAH/armIraqP2W.html. The tilt toward Saddam Hussein was finally enshrined in President Reagan's National Security Directive 114 on November 26, 1983.

8. Patrick Tyler, "Officers Say U.S. Aided Iraq in War Despite Use of Gas," *New York Times*, August 18, 2002.

9. Rumsfeld is known to have made at least one more visit to Baghdad, in early 1984.

10. Text of Howard Teicher, "The Teicher Affidavit: Iraq-Gate," Information Clearing House, January 31, 1995, http://www.informationclearinghouse.info/article1413.htm.

11. Ibid.

12. See "Chemical Weapons Program: History," Federation of American Scientists, http://www.fas.org/nuke/guide/iraq/cw/program.htm.

13. The purpose of the air-exclusion zones, also called "no-fly zones," proclaimed by the United States, Britain, and France was to provide humanitarian relief to the north and south. They were not authorized by the United Nations or sanctioned by a Security Council resolution. The UN secretary general at the time called them illegal. In 1998 France announced that it would no longer participate in policing these zones.

14. Interview with David Kay, *NewsHour*, PBS, October 2, 2003, http://www.pbs.org/newshour/bb/middle_east/july-dec03/kay_10-02.html.

15. Hussein Kamal later decided to return to Iraq under pressure from his wife, Saddam Hussein's daughter. He was murdered on his return.

16. See John Prados, ed., *The Curveball Affair*, National Security Archive Briefing Book no. 234 (Washington, DC: George Washington University, November 5, 2007).

17. "Curveball Revealed," *60 Minutes*, CBS, November 4, 2007.

18. To gauge the mind-set of George W. Bush and Tony Blair, see, for example, details of a secret memo about their meeting on January 31, 2003. The contents of the memo were published in the book *Lawless World: The Whistle-Blowing Account of How Bush and Blair Are Taking the Law into Their Own Hands* by distinguished British law pro-

fessor Philippe Sands (New York: Penguin, 2006) and discussed in the *Guardian* and the *New York Times*. See Don Van Natta, "Bush Was Set On Path to War, British Memo Says," *New York Times*, March 27, 2006; and Richard Norton-Taylor, "Blair-Bush Deal Before Iraq War Revealed in Secret Memo," *Guardian*, February 3, 2006. During the meeting, Bush said he would invade Iraq even if the UN inspectors found no weapons of mass destruction, the bombing of Iraq would begin around March 10, 2003, and he thought it unlikely that internecine war would break out between the different religious and ethnic groups in Iraq. Blair told Bush that a second UN resolution would be an "insurance policy" providing "international cover, including with the Arabs" if anything went wrong with the military campaign.

19. After General Tommy Franks infamously said, "We don't do body counts," the work fell on private organizations like Iraq Body Count, an Oxford Research Group project (http://www.iraqbodycount.org/), and the Randolph Bourne Institute's online facility AntiWar.com (http://www.antiwar.com/casualties/), which put the estimated number of Iraqi deaths until March 2008—the fifth anniversary of the invasion—at more than a million. Iraq Body Count is a research group made up of American and British academics and activists. It admits that its figures of civilian deaths attributable to coalition and insurgent military action are an undercount because of its stringent requirement for each death to be recorded only when it is reported in the media. Many deaths remain unreported.

20. It took the American forces until December 13, 2003, to capture Saddam Hussein at the small town of al-Dawr, near his stronghold, Tikrit. He was executed after a long and controversial trial three years later.

21. "Shock and Awe Campaign Underway in Iraq," CNN, March 22, 2003.

22. See Greg Palast, "Unreported: The Zarqawi Invitation," *Greg Palast: Journalism and Film*, http://www.gregpalast.com/unreported-the-zarqawi-invitation/.

23. Toby Dodge, "Staticide in Iraq," *Le Monde Diplomatique*, February 2007.

24. See Jonathan Steele, *Defeat: Why America and Britain Lost Iraq* (London: I. B. Taurus, 2007).

Chapter 6. Human Rights in Acute Crisis

1. See Nora Boustany, "Nations Use Fear to Distract from Rights Abuses, Group Says," *Washington Post*, May 24, 2007.

2. Kenneth Roth, "Despots Masquerading as Democrats," Human Rights Watch World Report 2008, 1.

3. According to Amnesty International USA, "habeas corpus" in Latin means "holding the body." People detained by the United States, either in or outside the country, are permitted to file a writ of habeas corpus in courts to seek relief from unlawful detention. It is an essential feature of democratic and constitutional governance and of international human rights law.

4. Peter Linebaugh, *The Magna Carta Manifesto: Liberties and Commons for All* (Berkeley: University of California Press, 2008), 26.

5. Ibid., 37.

6. This quote is sometimes also attributed to William Gladstone, the nineteenth-century British statesman and prime minister.

7. The Gulag was a system of detention and transit camps and prisons in the Soviet Union, where political prisoners and criminals were kept. The Gulag became a familiar

name with the publication of Aleksandr Solzhenitsyn's book *The Gulag Archipelago* in the West in 1973 (New York: Basic Books, 1997). In the opening chapter of his book, "Arrest," Solzhenitsyn described how it feels when someone is seized by shadowy individuals, about whom the victim knows nothing, and has no clue as to what lies ahead: "Arrest! Need it be said that it is a breaking point in your life. A bolt of lightning which has scored a direct hit on you." See page 3.

8.   "President Bush's Statement Regarding Secret Detention Centers in the EU," Council on Foreign Relations, September 6, 2006, http://www.cfr.org/publication/15060/president_bushs_statement_regarding_secret_detention_centers_in_the_eu.html.

9.   Despite strong opposition and recriminations, the British government pushed through the House of Commons legislation to increase detention without charge for terrorist suspects from twenty-eight to forty-two days in May 2008. A growing body of opponents complained that the use of loosely defined and hastily passed laws amounted to unwarranted and illegal curtailment of civil rights, citing, among other reasons, that the twenty-eight-day detention period had never been used in full. The House of Lords later defeated the measure, and the government dropped the bill.

10. For example, see "Dalai Lama Urged to Truly Not Support 'Tibetan Independence,'" Chinese news agency Xinhua, November 6, 2008.

11. See Ewen MacAskill, "Manual Exposes Divide and Rule Tactics at Camp Delta," *Guardian*, November 15, 2007; Reuters, "Guantanamo Operating Manual Posted on Internet," November 14, 2007.

12. The Council of Europe, founded in 1949, is an international organization with particular responsibility for the maintenance of human rights and democratic standards in Europe. At its heart are the European Convention of Human Rights, derived from the Universal Declaration, and the European Court of Human Rights. Its legal status is recognized under public international law. See Dick Marty, *Secret Detentions and Illegal Transfers of Detainees Involving Council of Europe Member-States: Second Report* (Strasbourg Cedex: Committee on Legal Affairs and Human Rights, Council of Europe, June 7, 2007), 4.

13. Ibid., 18–22; and Dick Marty, interview with Channel 4, UK, June 7, 2007.

14. George W. Bush and Tony Blair, news conference at the White House, July 18, 2003.

15. See Clive Stafford Smith, *Bad Men: Guantanamo Bay and the Secret Prisons* (London: Phoenix, 2007), 174–78 and 181–83; and Joel Campagna, "The Enemy?" *Dangerous Assignments*, Fall–Winter 2006, 56–60.

16. Reprieve, "U.S. Government Must Reveal Information about Prison Ships Used for 'Terror Suspects,'" press release, June 2, 2008.

17. Reprieve, "USS Bataan," http://www.reprieve.org.uk/ussbataan.

18. Duncan Campbell and Richard Norton-Taylor, "US Accused of Holding Terror Suspects on Prison Ships," *Guardian*, June 2, 2008.

19. *United States of America/Yemen: Secret Detention in CIA "Black Sites,"* Amnesty International, November 2005, http://www.amnesty.org/en/library/asset/AMR51/177/2005/en/413e36cb-d493-11dd-8a23-d58a49c0d652/amr511772005en.pdf.

20. Reprieve, "Ibn al Sheikh al libi," http://www.reprieve.org.uk/ibnalsheikhallibi.

21. For Binyam's story, see Smith, *Bad Men*, 49–80. See page 79 in particular for some interesting observations by the author.

22. "Interrogation Log: Detainee 063," *Time*, March 3, 2006.

23. Philippe Sands, "The Al Qahtani Debacle," *Bill Moyers Journal*, May 16, 2008; and

Philippe Sands, *Torture Team: Deception, Cruelty and the Compromise of Law* (London: Allen Lane, 2008).

24. Al-Qahtani was sometimes described by the Bush administration as the "twentieth hijacker," as though he were a reserve player on a team, despite the fact that he did not enter the United States. The administration claimed he was denied entry to America in August 2001.

25. Center for Constitutional Rights press release, February 11, 2008.

26. Antonio Taguba, "Key Excerpts from the Taguba Report," MSNBC, May 3, 2004. The report was not meant for public release, but it was leaked. For the catalogue of abuses in the full report, see *Article 15-6 Investigation of the 800th Military Police Brigade*, 16–17.

27. See Philip Gourevitch and Errol Morris, "Exposure," *New Yorker*, March 24, 2008, http://www.newyorker.com/reporting/2008/03/24/080324fa_fact_gourevitch.

28. Ibid, 4.

29. See R. Jeffrey Smith and Josh White, "General Granted Latitude at Prison: Abu Ghraib Used Aggressive Tactics," *Washington Post*, June 12, 2004.

30. Gourevitch and Morris, "Exposure," 4.

31. To gain a broad understanding, see Sands, *Torture Team:*, in particular the memo dated November 27, 2002, by General Counsel William Haynes and the note by Defense Secretary Donald Rumsfeld (p. 4). See also Sands, *Lawless World*.

Chapter 7. Rebuke of History

1. The tribesmen's number exceeded 100,000.

2. The collapse of the Berlin Wall and the fall of Communist regimes in Poland, Bulgaria, Romania, and Czechoslovakia all occurred in late 1989.

3. For example, Afghanistan, Iraq, Syria, Libya, and Ethiopia.

4. "Joint Declaration," U.S.-Russia Summit, Camp David, February 1, 1992, in NATO-Russia Archive, Berlin Information Center for Trans-Atlantic Security, http://www.bits.de.

5. The coup attempt (August 19-21, 1991) was carried out by a hard-line faction in the Soviet Communist Party, the KGB, and military officers, who all wanted to thwart the signing of a new union treaty devolving more power to the republics as part of Gorbachev's reforms. The attempt was badly conceived, badly planned, and poorly executed. It failed, bringing an end to the Communist Party and accelerating the collapse of the Soviet state.

6. Michael Beschloss and Strobe Talbott, *At the Highest Levels: The Inside Story of the End of the Cold War* (Boston: Little, Brown, 1993), 443.

7. For two authoritative estimates, see Amy F. Woolf, "Nuclear Weapons in the Former Soviet Union: Location, Command and Control," Issue Brief 91144, Congressional Research Service, November 1996, http://www.fas.org/spp/starwars/crs/91-144.htm; and Jeremiah Sullivan, "The Legacy of Nuclear Weapons," *Swords and Plowshares* 7, no. 2 (Winter 1992–93): 14–17.

8. Russia had 7,327 long-range strategic weapons, Ukraine, 1,568, Kazakhstan, 1,360, and Belarus, 54.

9. Sullivan, "Legacy of Nuclear Weapons."

10. The term "strategic partnership" also suggested that there would continue to be areas of competing interests for both Russia and the United States.

11. Sullivan, "Legacy of Nuclear Weapons."

12. Additional information revealed in 1993 suggested that Russia had twelve hundred tons of enriched uranium—more than twice the amount originally thought.

13. See "Joint Russian-American Declaration on Defense Conversion," Second Bush-Yeltsin Summit, Washington, DC, June 17, 1992, in NATO-Russia Archive, Berlin Information Center for Trans-Atlantic Security, http://www.bits.de.

14. The Soviet Threat Reduction Act was sponsored by Senator Sam Nunn (D-GA) and Senator Richard Lugar (R-IN). It was renamed after the collapse of the USSR as the Cooperative Threat Reduction Program.

15. "A Short History of Threat Reduction," *Arms Control Today*, June 2003, http://www.armscontrol.org/act/2003_06/luongohoehn_june03.asp.

16. Susan Koch, "Cooperative Threat Reduction: Reducing Weapons of Mass Destruction," *USIA Electronic Journal* 3, no. 3 (July 1998), http://usinfo.state.gov/journals/itps/0798/ijpe/pj38koch.htm.

17. "Short History of Threat Reduction."

18. START I, signed on July 31, 1991, was originally between the United States and the Soviet Union. On May 23, 1992, America and the four nuclear-capable successor states to the USSR (Russia, Ukraine, Belarus, and Kazakhstan) concluded the Lisbon Protocol, which made all five nations party to START I. See "START I at a Glance," Fact Sheet, Arms Control Association, January 2009, http://www.armscontrol.org/factsheets/start1.asp.

19. Iraq invaded Kuwait in August 1990, and the emirate was freed from occupation in a U.S.-led military campaign in early 1991. Thereafter, containment of Iraq in the region was to become a greater priority for America.

20. See George H. W. Bush, "State of the Union" (Washington, DC, January 1991).

21. Walter LaFeber, *America, Russia and the Cold War, 1945–2000*, 9th ed. (New York: McGraw-Hill, 2002), 359.

22. See Anthony Lake, "From Containment to Enlargement" (speech given at the School of Advanced International Studies, Johns Hopkins University, Washington, DC, September 21, 1993), http://highered.mcgraw-hill.com/olc/dl/35282/14_1_lake.html.

23. See Strobe Talbott, *The Russia Hand: A Memoir of Presidential Diplomacy* (New York: Random House, 2003), 38. A former Rhodes Scholar with Clinton at Oxford, Talbott was appointed ambassador-at-large and later deputy secretary of state by President Clinton.

24. The population of Kandahar in 1994 was about 250,000. Kandahar, an important market town, has road links to Kabul and Herat, near the Iranian border, and the Central Asian republics of the former Soviet Union. Kandahar and Peshawar in Pakistan's North-West Frontier Province are regarded as the principal cities of the Pashtun people.

25. Pakistani journalist, Ahmed Rashid, has written extensively on the Taliban. For example, see his book, *Taliban: The Story of the Afghan Warlords* (London: Pan Books, 2001), 21; "Afghanistan: Ending the Policy Quagmire," *Journal of International Affairs* 54, no. 2 (Spring 2001), 395–410; and "The Taliban: Exporting Extremism," *Foreign Affairs* 78, no. 6 (November/December 1999), 22–35.

26. The four schools of Islamic law that evolved in the ninth century were Hanafi, Maliki, Shafi, and Hanbali. See Rashid, *Taliban*, 83–92.

27. One-time foreign minister Mohammad Ghaus lost an eye and governor of Kandahar Mullah Mohammad Hasan and mayor of Kabul Abdul Majid each lost a leg. See ibid., 17–18.

28. See "Finally a Talkative Talib: Origins and Membership of the Students' Movement," February 20, 1995, in *The Taleban File*, National Security Archive Briefing Book no. 97 (Washington, DC: George Washington University, September 11, 2003).

29. In October 1994 Babar accompanied the ambassadors of six countries (the United States, Britain, Spain, Italy, China, and South Korea) in a land convoy that traveled from Pakistan to Herat in western Afghanistan. Pakistani officials from the departments of Railways, Highways, Telecommunications, and Electricity were with them. According to Ahmed Rashid, the journey was undertaken without informing the Kabul government. See Rashid, *Taliban*, 27, 251.

30. Conscious of the need to establish their own role, ISI officers had discreetly traveled to Herat in September 1994 to "survey" the road.

31. See Rashid, *Taliban*, 27.

32. Rashid, who has proven contacts in the Pakistani military, quotes his sources as saying that the Spin Buldak dump had approximately 18,000 Kalashnikov rifles and 120 artillery pieces, as well as ammunition. See Rashid, *Taliban*, 27. See also "[Excised] Believe Pakistan Is Backing Taliban," December 6, 1994, in *Taliban File*.

33. The then-head of the ISI, Lt. Gen. Javed Ashraf Qazi, was said to have told the Americans that his agency had "no role in supporting the Taliban." He said he had "strongly recommended to Prime Minister Bhutto" that the group not be supported in any way, but the interior minister had become the "principal patron of the Taliban." See "[Excised] Believe Pakistan Is Backing the Taliban."

34. Colonel Imam was described as the most prominent ISI field officer in the region, operating under cover as Pakistan's consul general in Herat. The Taliban commanders who were with the convoy were Mullah Borjan and Mullah Turabi. See Rashid, *Taliban*, 28.

35. For a summary of the ISI's problems at the time, see Rashid, "Pakistan and the Taliban," 84–86.

36. The army chief, Gen. Abdul Waheed; the head of military intelligence, Lt. Gen. Ali Kuli Khan; and all ISI field officers collaborating with the Taliban were Pashtuns.

37. President Rabbani and Masoud were both Tajik.

38. Najibullah's brother, Shahpur Ahmadzai, was chief of security at the presidential palace before his fall.

Chapter 8. Dimensions of Failure

1. Patrick Cockburn, "Iraq: Violence Is Down—But Not Because of America's Surge," *Independent*, September 14, 2008.

2. See "President Bush's Speech to the Israeli Parliament," Boston.Com, May 15, 2008, http://www.boston.com/news/nation/washington/articles/2008/05/15/text_of_president_bushs_speech_to_the_israeli_parliament/.

3. See "Abbas Pledge on 'Catastrophe' Day," *BBC News*, May 15, 2008, http://news.bbc .co.uk/1/hi/world/middle_east/7401892.stm.

4. For press reaction in the Arab world, see "Bush Speech Angers Arab Press," *BBC Online News*, May 16, 2008, http://news.bbc.co.uk/2/hi/middle_east/7404499.stm.

5. See "King, Bush Discuss Middle East," *Jordan Times*, January 13, 2008, http://www.jordanembassyus.org/new/newsarchive/2008/01132008001.htm.
6. See "Bush's 'Israel Bias' Angers Abbas," *BBC News*, May 18, 2008.
7. Dean Baker, *Recession Looms for the US Economy in 2007* (Washington, DC: Center for Economic and Policy Research, November 2006).

Chapter 9. Power Without Prudence

1. South Africa, Libya, and Vietnam also voted against the draft resolution discussed on July 11, 2008, in the Security Council.
2. Experts say it is impossible to calculate the precise amount because the war was financed in large part through emergency supplemental bills, which are not included in the U.S. federal budget. See Ron Sherer, "How US Is Deferring War Costs," *Christian Science Monitor*, January 16, 2007, http://www.csmonitor.com/2007/0116/p01s01-usfp.html.
3. World Prison Brief, International Center for Prison Studies, King's College, London University, 2009, http://www.kcl.ac.uk/depsta/law/research/icps/worldbrief/wpb_stats.php.
4. "Over 80m Americans Had No Health Insurance 2002 to 2003," *Medical News Today*, August 22, 2004, http://www.medicalnewstoday.com/articles/12370.php.
5. Jane Perlez and Robert F. Worth, "Attacks Traced to Two from Pakistan," *New York Times*, December 5, 2008.
6. See "US Confirms Saudi Role in Talks with Taliban," *Dawn*, November 25, 2009; also, "Holbrooke Confirms Saudi Role in Talks with Taliban," *The Nation*, November 25, 2009.

Epilogue

1. See "President Obama's Inaugural Address," January 20, 2009, in Appendix F.
2. Executive Order 13941, "Ensuring Lawful Interrogations," White House, http://www.whitehouse.gov/the_press_office/EnsuringLawfulInterrogations/.
3. "Barack Obama's 2002 Speech Against the Iraq War," http://obamaspeeches.com/001-2002-Speech-Against-the-Iraq-War-Obama-Speech.htm.
4. "Remarks by the President in Celebration of Nowruz," White House, March 20, 2009, http://www.whitehouse.gov/the_press_office/Videotaped-Remarks-by-The-President-in-Celebration-of-Nowruz/.
5. See Helen Cooper and Thom Shanker, "Aides Say Obama's Aims Elevate Afghan War," *New York Times*, January 27, 2009.
6. Richard Holbrooke interview, PBS, *NewsHour*, February 18, 2009.
7. See "Obama on AIG Rage, Recession, Challenges," CBS, *Sixty Minutes*, March 22, 2009.
8. Brian Knowlton, "Terror in America / 'We're Going to Smoke Them Out': President Airs His Anger," *New York Times*, September 19, 2001.

Bibliographic Essay

Few other assignments have impelled me more and presented me with such odds as writing this book. The horror of September 11, 2001, was hard to imagine until the moment it happened, but what followed was equally unthinkable. The attacks on the World Trade Center and the Pentagon were historic events that triggered a major world crisis. The smoke and dust of any great crisis can obscure critical details. Subsequent events acquire their own momentum, leading to unpredictable consequences. After 9/11, several important aspects of the events on that day lost the recognition they deserve. We should not fail to remind ourselves that the 9/11 attacks killed people of many countries, including hundreds of Pakistanis, Arabs, and Muslims from other nations. They were innocent victims, as were those many millions, all but a tiny number of them Muslims, who suffered in the subsequent war on terror. Any honest attempt to write history must include these aspects of George W. Bush's presidency.

While writing this book, the odds against me were formidable. I salute those activists, researchers, and writers who struggled harder and showed me the way. On the one hand, there was a determined, often overwhelming, official campaign of disinformation using modern media; on the other hand, there were ever-increasing restrictions on, and suppression of, reliable information. The National Security Archive at George Washington University in Washington, and organizations like Amnesty International, Human Rights Watch,

Reprieve, the American Civil Liberties Union, the Center for Public Integrity, and many others have striven to get to the truth throughout the past decade. My task would have been many times harder without them.

From the onset of the war on terror, the Bush administration displayed strong resistance to releasing information about civilian casualties—deaths in particular. The online project, Cursor, started by Marc Herold, a professor at the University of New Hampshire, filled the gap. Numbers provided by his project helped me put the loss of life in U.S.-led bombing raids in the initial weeks of the war in Afghanistan into context. Professor Herold's project was run on a meager budget until October 2008, when it became a victim of the economic crisis. But the service it had already provided was priceless. I am more grateful than I can say to Marc Herold and his team.

Also against numerous odds, the American Civil Liberties Union, Amnesty International, and Human Rights Watch ensured a steady flow of information and comment on abductions, detention, torture, and curtailment of individual liberties. I am thankful to them too.

The examination in chapter 1 of the controversial victory of George W. Bush against Al Gore in the November 2000 presidential election is derived from the archives of the Federal Election Commission, CNN, and the Northwestern University School of Law. A variety of news sources, among them broadcast media like the BBC, CNN, ABC, and Al Jazeera, as well as periodicals such as the *New York Times*, the *Washington Post*, *Time* magazine, and the *American Spectator*, were useful in developing an overview of the election campaigns of 2000, 2004, and 2008.

Several experts have linked the invasion of Iraq with America's dependence on Middle Eastern oil. In his January 2006 State of the Union address, President Bush himself acknowledged that the country was reliant on oil supplies from unstable parts of the world. The book *Addicted to Oil: America's Relentless Drive for Energy Security*, by Ian Rutledge (London: I. B. Taurus, 2006), and the memoir of the former chairman of the U.S. Federal Reserve, Alan Greenspan, *The Age of Turbulence: Adventures in a New World* (New York: Penguin, 2007), serialized in the *Times* of London, were helpful in the examination of the link between oil and American foreign policy.

A number of sources were beneficial in writing chapter 4, which looks at military operations by U.S.-led forces immediately after the invasion of

Afghanistan and the circumstances in which Osama bin Laden, his al Qaeda associates, and senior Taliban leaders escaped to sanctuaries inside Pakistan. Of particular help were documents made available by the Avalon Project of Yale Law School; articles in *Newsweek* and the *Christian Science Monitor*; the study by Cyrus Hodes and Mark Sedra, *The Search for Security in Post-Taliban Afghanistan* (Adelphi Paper 391, London: International Institute of Strategic Studies/Routledge, 2007); and *Jane's Intelligence Digest* on the security situation in Afghanistan and Pakistan.

For a general view of Pakistan's strategic interest in Afghanistan and the role of its military intelligence in the Afghan war, I turned to Shaun Gregory's *The ISI and the War on Terrorism* (Bradford, UK: Pakistan Security Research Unit, Department of Peace, University of Bradford, January 24, 2008), Brig. Mohammad Yousaf and Mark Adkin's *Afghanistan: The Bear Trap* (Barnsley, UK: Leo Cooper, 2001), and Frédéric Grare's "Pakistan: The Myth of an Islamic Peril" (Policy Brief 45, Washington, DC: Carnegie Endowment for International Peace, February 2006), among other sources. For an authoritative view of the Afghan crisis toward the end of the Bush presidency, I found *Resolving the Pakistan-Afghanistan Stalemate* by Barnett Rubin and Abubakar Siddiqui (Special Report, Washington, DC: U.S. Institute of Peace, October 2006), useful.

For an explanation of the invasion of Iraq and its consequences, the archive of the Federation of American Scientists on the Iraqi chemical weapons program proved beneficial. National Security Archive Briefing Book no. 234, *The Curveball Affair*, edited by John Prados (Washington, DC: George Washington University, November 5, 2007), revealed details of how Western intelligence was misled into believing claims about Saddam Hussein's weapons of mass destruction by an Iraqi national whose real motive was to find asylum in the West. The CBS investigation program *60 Minutes*, too, was helpful. To gauge the mind-set of George W. Bush and British prime minister Tony Blair, I turned to *Lawless World: America and the Making and Breaking of Global Rules,* by Philippe Sands (London: Alan Lane, 2005), and details of a secret memo about a meeting between Bush and Blair.

The discussion of the human rights crisis benefited from a number of sources. Most important were reports by Amnesty International and the

Council of Europe and the book *Bad Men: Guantanamo Bay and the Secret Prisons*, by Clive Stafford Smith (London: Phoenix, 2007). The interrogation log of Detainee 063 revealed by *Time* magazine (March 3, 2006) and Smith's book provided glimpses of torture techniques used on people kept at the Guantánamo Bay detention camp and other secret prisons. The Taguba Report (*Article 15-6 Investigation of the 800th Military Police Brigade*, May 2004), the official investigation into the regime of abuse at Iraq's Abu Ghraib prison, was of immense value. It provided a definitive verdict by a U.S. general who investigated the conduct of his own country's armed forces and found them inadequate in upholding the law. Despite attempts to suppress the report, it was leaked in 2004. Maj. Gen. Antonio Taguba was forced out of the military in January 2007. The following year, Taguba wrote the preface to a report by Physicians for Human Rights on prisoner abuse and torture in American military prisons in which he accused the Bush administration of committing war crimes. And to see it all in the context of the historical development of individual liberties over centuries, I turned to *The Magna Carta Manifesto: Liberties and Commons for All*, by Peter Linebaugh (Berkeley: University of California Press, 2008).

The war to overthrow the Taliban in Afghanistan was not about oil. It is, however, easier to see the invasion of Iraq, the broader war on terror, the extent of U.S. support for Israel, and Bush's support for Israel's war on Gaza as part of a grand strategy to dominate the oil-rich Middle East by military means. That grand strategy is described in the Project for the New American Century's "Statement of Principles" (Washington, DC, June 3, 1997). This organization was set up in 1997 with a view to ending the marginalization of the Republican Party and winning power three years later. The Project's manifesto provides a frame against which the conduct of the Bush administration can be evaluated.

Index